Template for Leadership

Template for Leadership

The Biblical Perspective

William Chauke

RESOURCE *Publications* • Eugene, Oregon

TEMPLATE FOR LEADERSHIP
The Biblical Perspective

Copyright © 2020 William Chauke. All rights reserved. Except for brief quotations in critical publications or reviews, no part of this book may be reproduced in any manner without prior written permission from the publisher. Write: Permissions, Wipf and Stock Publishers, 199 W. 8th Ave., Suite 3, Eugene, OR 97401.

Resource Publications
An Imprint of Wipf and Stock Publishers
199 W. 8th Ave., Suite 3
Eugene, OR 97401

www.wipfandstock.com

PAPERBACK ISBN: 978-1-7252-7375-7
HARDCOVER ISBN: 978-1-7252-7376-4
EBOOK ISBN: 978-1-7252-7377-1

Manufactured in the U.S.A.   06/02/20

Unless otherwise stated all Scripture quotations are taken from The Holy Bible, New International Version® NIV® Copyright© 1973, 1978, 1984, 2011 by Biblica, Inc. ™ Used by permission. All rights reserved worldwide.

Scripture quotations marked KJV are taken from The Holy Bible, King James Version® (KJV®). Copyright © 2002 by Barbour Publishing, Inc. Used by permission. All rights reserved.

Contents

Preface | vii

Acknowledgements | ix

1. There Is Nothing New under the Sun | 1
2. God's Template for Leadership | 3
3. Jesus Christ: The Model of Leadership | 15
4. The Call to Leadership: The Case of Moses | 50
5. The Call to Leadership: The Case of Paul | 62
6. The Call to Leadership: The Case of Joshua | 77
7. The Call to Leadership: The Case of Joseph | 83

A Valedictory Note | 97

Bibliography | 99

Preface

DURING THE SECOND SEMESTER of 2014, I dropped out from a PhD programme in Governance and Leadership, at the University of Lusaka, Zambia due to circumstances beyond my control. Little did I know then that God would enable me to pick up the broken pieces and move on, albeit in a different direction, a few years down the line. Little did I know then that as I was reviewing the literature in preparation for my thesis, God was preparing me for bible study, to facilitate my authorship in Christian leadership. I have indeed integrated some of the ideas on leadership acquired through the PhD programme, although I have now looked at them through a 'Christ-centric' lens, in line with my new calling.

At the beginning of 2017, God gave me a new vision and call for my life, and I immediately developed an intimate interest in studying the word of God and in meditation that have also resulted in continual revelation. One of the ministries I have been called to is the teaching of the word through writing. "Template for Leadership: The Biblical Perspective," is one of the products of this writing ministry.

The Holy Spirit revealed to me that there was nothing new under the sun, since everything-including good leadership-originates from God. I was then urged to write a book on leadership based on biblical insights and best practice, in order to provide guidance not only for church leaders, but for all leaders on godly leadership principles; so that God's kingdom comes and his will is done on earth as it is in heaven (Matthew 6:10). This book

Preface

will therefore serve as a valuable resource on leadership for both church based and circular leaders.

The current book draws from the example of God, the example of Jesus Christ, and of others like Joseph; Moses, Joshua, and Paul, who were called into leadership as recorded in the bible; in order to show good leadership styles, best leadership practices, and the underlying guiding principles that today's leaders need to embrace in order to become more effective.

Acknowledgements

FIRST AND FOREMOST, I would like to thank our Lord and Savior, Jesus Christ; for making me a vessel of honor, by calling me to the Teaching Ministry of which this book is one testament.

Second, I would like to extend my gratitude to my late father, for having brought me up in a Christian home. May his dear soul rest in eternal peace!

I also want to thank all the pastors and men of God—too numerous to mention by name-who nurtured me in the Christian walk.

Last, and by no means least, I want to thank my dear wife Grace for bearing with me as I burnt the "midnight oil" in the writing of this book.

1

There Is Nothing New under the Sun

LEADERSHIP WAS INITIATED BY God, modelled by Jesus, and replicated by man across all dispensations. Whenever God wanted to chart a new course in history or introduce far-reaching developments in society, he would raise a man or woman, to identify with that vision. Indeed the word of God shows us that there is nothing new under the sun. See the Scripture below in that regard:

> What has been will be again, what has been done will be done again; there is nothing new under the sun.
> (Eccl 1:9, NIV)

As with everything else, there is nothing new under the sun; so the same goes for leadership.

Although leadership can be divided into two broad categories or approaches: participative and non-participative, this book will be devoted entirely to the former, since this resonates with God's heart for leadership.

Since God initiated leadership, we can draw useful lessons for ourselves by studying his word on good leadership as exercised by God, modelled by Jesus, and played out by anointed man and women throughout the ages. Indeed it is the above-mentioned pattern of leadership that can be used as a template by leaders today-since in addition to being participative-it is also godly. This

Template for Leadership

is the reason why this book is titled, "Template for Leadership: The Biblical Perspective."

As you read through this book, you will realise that the leadership styles-which we could also call peculiar leadership genres-used by the men and women God raised, mimic those used by God himself. This serves to underscore the fact that since man was created in the image and likeness of God, they should also embrace godly leadership practices, in order to truly represent that reality. And this equally applies to leaders in all fields of human endeavour, since all men were created in God's image or likeness!

Even in other fields of human endeavour, besides church ministry; the leadership styles that are more acceptable are of the participative variety, an indication that good leadership emanates from God.

It is my sincere prayer, that as you read this book, you will discover and embrace your own call to leadership. And if already a leader, it is also my sincere prayer that you will appreciate and faithfully embrace godly leadership practices, for your own growth and above all, to God's glory.

2

God's Template for Leadership

LEADERSHIP CAN BE DEFINED as the ability to influence others for the voluntary pursuit of organizational or institutional objectives. The voluntary pursuit of organisational or institutional objectives by followers is critical because it ensures sustainability, whether the leader is present or not since the followers would be totally sold out to the leaders' ideas. Buy-in or followership is the hallmark of leadership, because without followership, there can never be any leadership to talk about.

While leadership and management may not strictly speaking be interchangeable concepts since some junior employees of an organisation could also possess the ability to mobilise and influence others for specific ends, albeit in the short term. These ends usually have nothing to do with the strategic or long-term goals of the organisation; tending to be more or less of a self-serving, disruptive or of a trade unionist nature. Notwithstanding that, it is the people in management positions who are best suited to move their organisations, churches and or ministries in the direction of their desired vision. It is for this reason that God calls formal leaders, whenever there is a need to chart a new course in history.

The story of man's creation provides a compelling template for leadership in today's world. It is a template in the sense that

Template for Leadership

there is nothing new under the sun, as alluded to by the Scripture cited above.

For details on man's creation and its implications for leadership, see the Scripture below:

> Then God said, "Let us make mankind in our image, in our likeness that they may rule over the fish in the sea and the birds in the sky, over the livestock and all the wild animals, and over all the creatures that move along the ground." (Gen 1:26, NIV)

God the Father is the first personality and leader of the Holy Trinity or Godhead comprising the Father, the Son (Jesus Christ) and the Holy Spirit. As leader of the Godhead, God cast the vision of man's creation and then invited the other members to share in that vision. God is therefore the originator of visionary leadership.

If leadership wasn't meant to be shared, God would have just announced that he was going to create mankind, rather than proposing such action to the other members of the Holy Trinity.

God the Father was, therefore, initiating visionary leadership, by charting a new course in history through man's creation.

The lessons to be learnt by today's leaders from God's visionary leadership are as follows:

1. A leader is not a boss.
2. Good leadership says 'us' not 'I'; 'we' not 'me'.
3. Good leadership involves consultation rather than dictation.
4. Leaders should throw out of the window all dictatorial tendencies, since they are counterproductive and often result in contempt and resistance from fellow leaders and followers.
5. Without an ultimate strategic focus, people have no claim to visionary leadership.

The leadership principles implicit in the story of creation for leaders today are the following:

- Participation.
- Consultation.
- Having an ultimate strategic focus.

Participation and consultation are of crucial importance to leadership as they engender a sense of ownership of and loyalty to the decisions arrived at. Followers become more favourably disposed towards the leader in the future and as a result this increases their leadership clout.

The characteristic that sets apart a leader-especially a top leader—from others, is in their strategic orientation, because the essence of leadership lies in one's ability to take others to an envisioned future state or condition or to guide them towards the attainment of the vision, lest they get lost somewhere along the way. See the Scriptures below on the strategic nature of a vision:

> For the vision is of yet an appointed time, but at the end it shall speak . . . (Hab 2:3, KJV)

> Where there is no vision, the people perish . . . (Prov 29:18a, KJV)

An effective leader is therefore expected not to lose sight of the bigger picture.

While being mindful of the day-to-day operations, an impactful leader should ultimately ensure that these serve as mere building blocks for the envisioned future state or condition. As they 'see the trees,' good leaders should never lose sight of the 'entire forest!' Strategic thinking is therefore the recipe for success for the leader.

Top leaders should ensure that only programmes that feed into the existing vision are implemented, because leaders will only be rewarded for the successful execution of their God-given vision, hence the need for a strategic focus. Activities that do not feed into the vision should be deliberately avoided. Paul aptly used the metaphor of a serving soldier to illustrate this point:

Template for Leadership

> No one serving as a soldier gets entangled in civilian affairs, but rather tries to please his commanding officer. (2 Tim 2:4, NIV)

In other Scriptures, Paul urged faithful service, when he said:

> I press on toward the goal to win the prize for which God has called me heavenward in Christ Jesus. (Phil 3:14, NIV)

> We have different gifts according to the grace given us... if it is to lead, do it diligently... (Rom 12:6a; 8c, NIV)

Those who have been called to leadership, who serve faithfully, are indeed good stewards of their God-given gifts and they shall be handsomely rewarded in due course. Even in the circular world, those with leadership responsibilities who are diligent always meet their goals; thereby positioning themselves for appropriate rewards in due course.

Principles refer to ideal standards guiding leadership practices that are enduring in nature, in spite of changes in the environment. Strict adherence to stipulated principles has the potential of ensuring achievement of a leader's objectives, since principles tend to be acceptable, enduring, and are all-inclusive.

God's proposal for the creation of man to the Son and the Holy Spirit shows that godly leadership is never a loner's preserve, but a shared enterprise by actors who play complementary roles. By so doing, God was also initiating complementary leadership. God the Father is the initiator and originator of all developments in the universe, while the Son and the Holy Spirit support and run with those visions. Jesus Christ and the Holy Spirit are responsible for the execution of all heavenly visions.

Complementarity in leadership implies that there are two broad levels of leadership: visionary/strategic leadership and complementary/tactical/operational leadership.

Complementarity in leadership was initiated by God according to Genesis 1:26 cited in this book. And in the same vein, Paul advocated for the same in the body of Christ. This also subsumes church leaders, who constitute a pivotal part of that body. See the Scripture below for more details:

God's Template for Leadership

> For just as each of us has one body with many members, and all these members do not have the same function, so in Christ we, though many, form one body, and each member belongs to all the others. (Rom 12:4–5, NIV)

Complementarity in leadership is important because God gave us different gifts commensurate with our callings and or abilities. See the Scriptures below on this subject:

> We have different gifts according to the grace given to each of us. (Rom 12:6a, NIV)

Complementary leadership in the Godhead can be deduced from their diverse but complementary roles in man's salvation. God loved sinful mankind and entered into a covenant of redemption with Jesus to come and die in our stead on the cross of Calvary, so that only through faith would we receive the free gift of salvation. Additionally, it would be the Holy Spirit who would convict man of sin, in order to lead them to repentance so that they could access salvation and have their sins forgiven.

God initiated complementary leadership because it tends to create synergy within the leadership team. Synergy can be defined as a superior outcome that emanates from joint action by actors with different roles and or capabilities that are greater than the outcome resulting from the actions of independent and uncoordinated actors. See the Scriptures below that illustrate the complementarity of the Godhead in man's salvation:

> For God so loved the world that he gave his one and only Son, that whoever believes in him shall not perish but have eternal life. (John 3:16, NIV)

> He forgave us all our sins, having cancelled the charge of our legal indebtedness, which stood against us and condemned us; he has taken it away nailing it to the cross. (Col 2:13b–14, NIV)

> But when he, the Spirit of truth comes, he will guide you into all truth. (John 16:13b–14, NIV)

Template for Leadership

> When he comes, he will prove the world to be in the wrong about sin and righteousness and judgement: about sin because people do not believe in me ... (John 16:8–9, NIV)

So according to the last Scripture quoting Jesus cited above, it is the work of the Holy Spirit to draw mankind into believing in Jesus' atoning work at Calvary, thereby leading them to repentance.

Because all of us have not been called to be overall or visionary leaders, some have also been called to support and run with the vision as complementary leaders. The vision should of course be in line with sound doctrine to merit any support from complementary leaders, because a God-given vision should be efficacious. Moreover, to receive buy-in, visionary leaders should also possess team building attributes.

Complementary leaders could be anyone from junior pastor, deacon, elder or board member; depending on the church's organisational structure.

For the avoidance of confusion, there should be only one visionary in the church with the other top leadership team members running with that vision, as it is in heaven. This means that these leaders should complement and work in concert with the church or organisational leader. It is of course of prime importance to have one visionary leader, to preclude the emergence of diverse and potentially competing visions, as alluded to by the Scripture cited below:

> For God is not a God of disorder but of peace. (1 Cor 14:33a, NIV)

Visionary leaders could be anyone from pastor, teacher, evangelist, apostle or prophet according to the so-called five-fold ministry concept.

A vision is a leader's specific God-given mandate or assignment or calling. Visionary leaders are of course supposed to work in collaboration with complementary leaders in order to bring their vision to fruition.

The lessons to be learnt by today's leaders in respect of God's template of complementary leadership are as follows:

God's Template for Leadership

1. Leadership is a shared enterprise.
2. Leaders should be good team players.
3. There is division of labour in leadership (envisioning and complementing of the vision).
4. Coordinated leadership produces superior outcomes or synergy.

The principles implicit in complementary leadership that leaders today should embrace are the following:

- Cooperation.
- Role clarity.
- Building synergies or complementarity.

Where leaders work cooperatively, their energies are directed towards the achievement of set goals. And where leaders are clear about their respective roles, there is role clarity in terms of envisioning and execution/complementing, leading to the building of synergies due to the higher probability of non-overlapping weaknesses and or deficiencies in the leadership team.

The vision for man's creation was cast in clear and unambiguous terms, describing the course of action to be taken i.e. creation of man in God's likeness. The purpose or mission for man's creation was the devolution of authority to lead the management of the affairs of the world to man.

Visionary leadership therefore involves the casting of a compelling and worthwhile vision that should be clearly articulated for ease of buy-in. A good example of how to clearly communicate a vision is shown by the story of Habakkuk in the following Scripture:

> Then the LORD replied: "Write down the revelation and make it plain on tablets so that a herald may run with it."
> (Hab 2:2, NIV)

Please note that the word "revelation" is referred to as "vision" in the King James Version of the Holy Bible. Also note that a herald is someone sent to relay a message, who in the case of the leadership team, can be the complementary leader.

Template for Leadership

In order to realise one's vision, the visionary leader works in concert with complementary leaders to support and champion the vision with the followers. The complementary leaders are then given the responsibility of fashioning out and implementing relevant strategies to accomplish the given vision

Strategies can be defined as specific actions required to attain a certain goal and to achieve specific objectives.

The lessons that today's leaders can draw from God's visionary leadership are the following:

1. Overall leaders should have a clear vision.
2. Leaders should clearly articulate a worthy cause/vision.
3. Leadership involves the envisioning and execution of a given vision.
4. Leadership involves joint decision-making.

The principles for today's leaders that are implicit in God's visionary leadership are the following:

- Clear communication.
- Cooperation.
- Joint decision-making.

Visionary leaders are called upon to cultivate good communication skills to ensure buy-in of their vision. Leaders could do so through prayer for wisdom and continual guidance during all their interactions with others. They may also take communication courses.

For the avoidance of doubt, all organisations should write down their organisational vision in order to guide executive management in the formulation of relevant strategies for the achievement of the given vision.

Cooperation between visionary and complementary leaders creates unity of purpose among the leaders, thereby ensuring the successful execution of that vision. Joint decision-making creates a sense of ownership of all the decisions arrived at, thereby unlocking the commitment of all players in all planned courses of action.

The fact that man was eventually created shows God's influence with the other members of the Godhead, probably because he treated them as his equals who had to be consulted rather than being dictated to and by also clearly articulating his vision for man's creation as a worthy cause. As the initiator of visionary leadership, God proposed a far-reaching vision that would positively impact the leadership of world affairs; hence buy-in by our Lord and Saviour, Jesus Christ and the Holy Spirit.

The purpose of man's creation was to make him manager or leader over God's creation as his steward, as the Scripture below seems to suggest:

> You made them rulers over the works of your hands.
> (Ps 8:6, NIV)

As the above-cited Scripture indicates, being made in God's likeness means that man also has the capacity to emulate God in the leadership or 'rulership' of world affairs.

And in line with the above-mentioned role, man as faithful stewards, should be concerned about the welfare of all of God's creation, as God himself does. Principally, church or ministry leaders—as good stewards—should channel available resources to meet the social or physical needs of their congregants in addition to their spiritual needs, because:

> The LORD is a refuge for the oppressed, a stronghold in
> times of trouble. (Ps 9:9, NIV)

Good stewardship, in as far as foregoing one's comfort by channelling available resources to worthy causes such as meeting the needs of others, is one way of demonstrating sacrificial leadership.

Therefore, church leaders should be good stewards by encouraging the channelling of God-given church resources to worthy causes such as the welfare of the poor, widows and orphans. In any case, true worship that God cherishes is the following:

Template for Leadership

> Religion which God our Father accepts as pure and faultless is this: to look after orphans and widows in their distress and to keep one from being polluted by the world. (Jas 1: 27, NIV)

The lesson that today's leaders can learn about good stewardship is as follows:

1. Leaders should consistently pursue the benefit of others ahead of their own comfort.

The leadership principles that are implicit in good stewardship are the following:

- Selflessness.
- Social responsibility.

Leaders who are seen to be selfless and practice good social responsibility have the ability to inspire their followers and to gain their trust and loyalty, paving the way for the latter to cooperate in the former's projects and or programmes.

To wrap up, lessons that today's leaders can learn from the template of leadership provided by the Godhead, are as follows:

1. Overall leaders should be humble and consider other leaders as their equals.
2. Overall leaders should be diligent, clearly articulating their God-given vision for the church.
3. Overall leaders should not dictate the strategies or work programme of the church, in order to ensure unanimity as long as these are in sync with the church's vision.
4. Church leaders should complement each other rather than work at cross-purposes.
5. Visionary leaders should clearly communicate their vision to complementary leaders for their buy-in.
6. Church leaders should be team players since leadership should be a shared enterprise.

7. Church and or ministry leaders should be faithful stewards who should properly manage the affairs of their churches by among other things seeking to meet the physical needs of the disadvantaged among their members or wider society.
8. Business leaders should also embrace corporate social responsibility programmes to be worthy their salt.
9. Church leaders should take a leaf from the Godhead in their leadership practices as part of the Lord's Prayer suggests:

   > Your kingdom come, your will be done, on earth as it is in heaven. (Matt 6:10, NIV)

10. While being mindful of day-to-day operations, leaders should have an ultimate strategic focus to be impactful.

Churches, ministries and organisations could do well to adopt the above-mentioned leadership practices and to also espouse the corresponding leadership principles of:

- Humility.
- Diligence.
- Consultation.
- Complementarity.
- Clear communication.
- Stewardship.
- Cooperation.
- Social responsibility.
- Responsiveness.
- Strategic focus.

Embracing the above-mentioned leadership principles serves to endear leaders to co-leaders and followers as shown earlier in this chapter.

Being made in the likeness of God, means man was given dominion over the affairs of the earth just as God rules over the

Template for Leadership

affairs of the entire universe. Therefore, in similar vein, top church leaders have been given the mandate to cast the vision of the entire church or church ministry; while complementary leaders are responsible for supporting and executing the same vision.

Being made in the likeness of God also means that man is endowed with the capacity to emulate the leadership styles initiated by God. This capacity for godly leadership can be appreciated as one reads the word of God, and can be activated as one engages in prayer and meditation; which then leads to revelation.

Since leaders have an ultimate strategic focus, organisations should ensure that their top leaders formulate strategic plans and follow them through. For fairness' sake, leaders should be hired for fairly long enough periods, say five or ten years; since their performance is predicated on strategic rather than tactical or operational objectives. The renewal of leaders' contracts should also be performance based.

3

Jesus Christ

The Model of Leadership

JESUS CHRIST WAS THE perfect example and model of humility and servant leadership, which every leader should emulate. See the Scriptures cited below for further details on his humility and servant leadership style:

> Who being in very nature God, did not consider equality with God as something to be used to his own advantage; rather he made himself nothing by taking the very nature of a servant being made in human likeness. And being found in appearance as a man, he humbled himself by becoming obedient to death—even death on the cross. (Phil 2:6–8, NIV)

> All this took place to fulfil what the Lord had said through the prophet: 'the virgin will conceive and give birth to a son, and they will call him Immanuel' (which means "God with us" (Isaiah 7:14). (Matt 1:22–23, NIV)

The lessons for today's leaders from Jesus' example of humility and servant leadership are as follows:

1. Leaders should be humble.

Template for Leadership

2. Leaders should first and foremost be prepared to serve others before considering their own interests.

The leadership principles implicit in Jesus' example cited above are the following:

- Humility.
- Service.

Humility and service can earn the leader both the admiration and loyalty of their followers, who also become more favourably disposed to following the former in future endeavours. The reason why Christianity is the biggest religion in the world today is because of Jesus' humility and selfless service to humanity, when he laid down his life for the redemption of the world.

Jesus' washing of his disciples' feet is another compelling demonstration of the fact that he was the perfect model of servant leadership. This incident also served as a teachable moment for Jesus to impart the same virtue to his disciples. See the Scripture below for further details:

> After that he poured out water into a basin, and began to wash his disciples' feet, drying them with the towel wrapped around him . . ."You call me Teacher and Lord, and rightly so, for that is what I am. Now that I your Lord and Teacher have washed your feet, you also should wash one another's feet." (John 15:5, 13–14, NIV)

The lessons for today's leaders from Jesus' example of servant leadership through the washing of his disciples' feet are as follows:

1. Leaders should humble themselves before being exalted.
2. Leaders should be prepared to serve others and not expect to always being served.

The leadership principles implicit in Jesus' display of servant leadership in the above-mentioned incident are the following:

- Humility.
- Service.

Jesus Christ: The Model of Leadership

Humility and service serve to make leaders more acceptable to their followers. This in turn elicits the cooperation of followers in future endeavours.

When James and John, sons of Zebedee, came to Jesus asking for places of honor in his kingdom, he also took this as another teachable moment for imparting the tenets of servant leadership, of which he was the perfect example. See the Scripture below for further details:

> No so with you. Instead, whoever wants to become great among you must be your servant, and whoever wants to be first among you must be slave of all. For even the Son of Man did not come to be served, but to serve and to give his life as a ransom for many. (Mark 10:43–45, NIV)

The lessons that today's leaders can learn from the story of the sons of Zebedee are as follows:

1. Leaders should be humble.
2. Leadership positions should be used for the purpose of serving others.
3. Leadership is earned through hard work.
4. Leaders should be the greatest workers (servants), and should be prepared to put in long hours in order to inspire their followers to diligence.
5. Leaders should accept lowliness before 'loftiness'.
6. To be a great leader, one should have great humility.
7. Top leaders should teach complementary leaders good leadership styles and principles by-among other things-being able to identify relevant teachable moments for them.

The leadership principles emanating from the above-mentioned story are the following:

- Diligence.
- Service.
- Humility.

Template for Leadership

- Discipleship.

Church or ministry leaders today should be prepared to get their hands dirty (diligence) and do even menial tasks (serving) if this is what it takes to inspire diligence among their followers. Leaders who are humble embrace everyone, thereby gaining the acceptability and loyalty of everyone. Moreover, good leaders are those that mentor or disciple their followers.

Diligence and humility are therefore important pillars of leadership, because humble and diligent leaders, gain the respect and loyalty of their followers; resulting in their leadership clout increasing.

Indeed Jesus' example of servant leadership shows that 'the way up is through going down', because:

> Pride brings a person low, but the lowly in spirit gain honor. (Prov 29:23, NIV)

> . . . Those who exalt themselves will be humbled and those who humble themselves will be exalted. (Matt 23:12b, NIV)

> All of you clothe yourselves with humility toward one another, because, "God opposes the proud but shows favor to the humble. Proverbs 3:34. (1 Pet 5:5b–6, NIV)

Having endured humiliation, Jesus, once glorified; was greatly exalted:

> Therefore God exalted him to the highest place and gave him the name that is above every name, that at the name Jesus, every knee should bow, in heaven and on earth and under the earth and every tongue acknowledge that Jesus Christ is Lord to the glory of God the Father. (Philippians 2:9–11, NIV)

> And God placed all things under his feet and appointed him to be head over everything for the church which is his body, the fullness of him who fills everything in every way. (Ephesians 1:22–23, NIV)

Jesus Christ: The Model of Leadership

When Jesus fed the Five Thousand, he was also demonstrating servant leadership in that it was him and his disciples actually serving people food, instead of the other way round, in line with conventional practice. See the Scriptures below for more details:

> As evening approached, the disciples came to him and said, "This is a remote place, and it is already getting late. Send the crowds away, so they can go to the villages and buy themselves food." Jesus replied, "They do not need to go away. You give them something to eat." (Matt 14:15, NIV)

> And he directed the people to sit down on the grass. Taking the five loaves and two fish and looking up to heaven, he gave thanks and broke the loaves. Then he gave them to his disciples, and the disciples gave them to the people. (Matt 14:19, NIV)

The feeding of the five thousand also shows that leaders should utilise available resources to cater for the physical needs of congregants and the wider society, in line with responsible stewardship. See the relevant Scripture below:

> "We have here only five loaves of bread and two fish," they answered. "Bring them here to me," he said. (Matt 14:17–18, NIV)

The feeding of five thousand men-excluding women and children—also serves to illustrate the power of generosity, in that as long as the disciples continued giving the people the pieces of bread and fish, these continued multiplying until all the people were fed; leaving behind twelve basketfuls of leftovers.

Indeed generosity is vital, because it is not a vain pursuit as one Scripture shows:

> Give and it will be given to you. A good measure, pressed down, shaken together and running over will be poured into your lap. For with the measure you use, it will be measured to you. (Luke 6:38, NIV)

Template for Leadership

The value of generosity lies in its multiplicative nature, because those who are in the habit of giving always receive much more than they would have given. And the more people continue to give, the more they continue to receive from God. And this equally applies to business leaders.

The feeding of the five thousand by Jesus has some implications for today's leaders, as follows:

1. Church leaders should minister to the total person-body, soul and spirit.
2. Church leaders should introduce compassionate ministries and or programmes to cater for the welfare needs of their congregants and the wider society.
3. Business leaders should also embrace corporate social responsibility programmes.
4. Leaders should be good stewards of God-given resources.
5. As long as church leaders continue giving to the needy, their churches will always have more than they need.

Through the feeding of the five thousand, Jesus was showing his disciples the way to go by demonstrating three leadership principles:

- Compassion.
- Stewardship.
- Social responsibility.

Leaders who are compassionate, generous and use available resources to meet the total needs of their congregants and the wider society are highly acceptable and influential.

Our Lord and Saviour, Jesus Christ taught his disciples the virtues of servant leadership, denouncing the pride of the teachers of the law and the Pharisees; who expected to be respected by all, and to be always served and honoured by all. The following Scriptures are very instructive in this regard:

Jesus Christ: The Model of Leadership

> Everything they do is done for people to see ... they love the place of honour at banquets and the most important seats in the synagogues. They love to be greeted with respect in the marketplaces and to be called, 'Rabbi' by others. (Matt 23:5a; 6–7, NIV)

> The greatest among you will be your servant. For those who exalt themselves will be humbled, and those who humble themselves will be exalted. (Matt 23:11–12, NIV)

Leaders today can draw some useful lessons from Jesus' above-mentioned admonition as follows:

1. Leaders should be humble i.e. the way "up" is through going "down."
2. Leadership is more about what one gives than about what one gets by virtue of their position.
3. Leaders should also be prepared to serve than expect to be served all the time.
4. Leaders should shake off the entitlement mentality.

The leadership principles implicit in Jesus' teachings cited above are the following:

- Humility
- Service

Humility is vital in that leaders who humble themselves are more likely than those with an entitlement mentality to gain the admiration, acceptance and loyalty of their followers. This will in turn enable leaders to positively influence followers along desired directions.

Service is also vital in the sense that it is, more often than not, the leaders who are prepared "to have their hands dirty" in order to meet the needs of others, who also earn the respect and loyalty of their followers.

Jesus taught in synagogues and everywhere he went, pointing the way to salvation, as the epitome of visionary leadership.

Template for Leadership

Visionary leaders always point for their followers the way to go, so they do not lose sight of the ultimate goal. See the Scriptures below on Jesus' role as a visionary leader:

> 'But you, Bethlehem, in the land of Judah, are by no means least among the rulers of Judah; for out of you will come a ruler who will shepherd my people Israel.' (Micah 5:2, 4). (Matt 2:6, NIV)

> From that time on Jesus began to preach, "Repent, for the kingdom of heaven has come near." (Matt 4:17, NIV)

The lesson for today's leaders from Jesus' example of visionary leadership, are as follows:

1. Leaders should always point the way of salvation to their followers or always remind them of their mandate.

The leadership principle implicit in Jesus' visionary leadership is that of:

- Clarity of vision.

Leaders who are clear about their vision and or mandate always steer their followers in the right direction.

Note that a shepherd is responsible for directing the flock to green pastures and for keeping it out of harm's way. By preaching, teaching and showing his audiences the way of salvation in order to escape impending punishment in hell, Jesus was indeed playing his role as the model of visionary leadership. Indeed preachers today should take a leaf from Jesus' example.

When Jesus sent out his disciples to preach and drive out demons and heal the sick, he seized the opportunity of turning the occasion into a teachable moment for his disciples in order for them to have passion for their work that goes beyond material benefits. In this, Jesus was teaching his disciples the way to go, as the model of visionary leadership. See the Scripture below for more information:

Jesus Christ: The Model of Leadership

> As you go proclaim this message: 'The kingdom of God has come near.' Heal the sick, raise the dead, cleanse those who have leprosy, drive out demons. Freely you have received; freely give. (Matt 10:7-8, NIV)

Jesus' injunction to his disciples served as a template for ministry for his disciples not to be motivated by material gain in their work, which incidentally equally applies to today's leaders. In similar vein, Peter also expressed similar sentiments when he declared that:

> Be shepherds of God's flock that is under your care, watching over them-not because you must, but because you are willing, as God wants you to be: not pursuing dishonest gain, but eager to serve. (1 Peter 5:2, NIV)

Paul, in line with Jesus' instruction to his disciples, demonstrated having faithfully embraced the same virtues when he asserted in the Scripture below that:

> Unlike so many, we do not peddle the word of God for profit. (2 Cor 2:17a, NIV)

Indeed Jesus' instruction to his disciples also addresses today's church leaders—some of whom charge a fee for counselling, healing and deliverance—not to do so, because as they themselves received spiritual gifts for free from God, they should also be a channel of healing and deliverance to others for free!

Four lessons that today's leaders can appropriate for themselves from Jesus' instruction to the disciples are as follows:

1. Visionary leaders should show complementary leaders the way to go.
2. Visionary leaders should identify teachable moments for their complementary leaders.
3. Church leaders should refrain from manipulating their followers for personal gain.
4. Leadership is more about what one gives to and not about what one gets out of ministry or from the organisation.

Template for Leadership

The above-mentioned instruction of Jesus to his disciples, can serve to instil four leadership principles:

- Service.
- Faithfulness.
- Selflessness.
- Commitment.

Leaders who serve faithfully, are selfless and are committed to their calling, endear themselves to their followers. They also please God who is their ultimate rewarder. Such leaders are acceptable to their followers who become more amenable to the leader's future suggestions.

Jesus' outstanding performance in his work in word and deed marked him as the epitome of visionary leadership as he remained focussed and highly motivated to accomplish his assignment on earth. See the Scripture below for your inspiration:

> Coming to his hometown he began teaching the people in their synagogues and they were amazed. "Where did this man get this wisdom and these miraculous powers?" they asked. (Matt 13:54, NIV)

The people of Nazareth in the Scripture cited above were referring to Jesus' work wherever he went, since he was being empowered by the Holy Spirit. Below, find one Scripture that attests to Jesus' outstanding ministry:

> And when the men of that place recognized Jesus, they sent word to all the surrounding country. People brought all their sick to him and begged him to let the sick just touch the edge of his cloak, and all who touched it were healed. (Matt 14:35–36, NIV)

Indeed, prophet Isaiah had prophesied about Jesus in the following Scripture:

> Here is my servant, whom I uphold, my chosen one in whom I delight; I will put my Spirit on him and he will bring justice to the nations. (Isa 42:1–2, NIV)

Jesus Christ: The Model of Leadership

The lessons that can be drawn from the Nazareth incident for today's leaders are three-fold:

1. Leaders with clarity of vision stand out of the crowd.
2. Church leaders who submit to the guidance of the Holy Spirit do exploits.
3. Non-church leaders who meticulously follow the vision and goals of their organisations perform better than those who don't, in terms of business outcomes.

The leadership principles implicit in the Nazarene incident are the following:

- Pursuit of excellence.
- Diligence.

Diligence and the pursuit of excellence by the leader inspire the followers to emulate them. Diligence and pursuit of excellence can also be considered as two pillars of success in whatever a leader sets out to do.

While visionary leaders show their followers the way to go, they also identify teachable moments to do so, just as our model of visionary leadership-Jesus Christ-did. On one occasion, when the disciples had forgotten to take bread along with them, he warned them against the teaching of the Pharisees and Sadducees, by using the metaphor of yeast. See the Scriptures below for more details:

> "Be careful," Jesus said to them. "Be on your guard against the yeast of the Pharisees and Sadducees." They discussed this among themselves and said, "Is it because we didn't bring any bread . . . How is it you don't understand I was not talking to you about bread?". . . Then they understood he was not telling them to guard against the yeast in bread, but against the teaching of the Pharisees and Sadducees. (Matt 16:6–7; 11a, 12, NIV)

Teachable moments that leaders could use to impart relevant virtues or values could be when followers are discussing topical issues or when a disgraceful incident has occurred in the church.

Template for Leadership

The use of popular metaphors and or clichés enables leaders to connect effectively with their follower's reality.

The lessons that today's leaders could appropriate for themselves from the 'bread-and-yeast' story are that:

1. Leaders should identify teachable moments for their followers.
2. Leaders should use familiar figures of speech/language in order to connect and communicate more effectively with their followers.

Through the above-mentioned story, Jesus was promoting the leadership principle of:

- Creating rapport (with followers).

The creation of rapport with one's audience ensures that a leader gains the ability to communicate more effectively.

Jesus Christ, as the model of visionary leadership, showed his disciples, the virtues of humility by using the metaphor of a little child. It was when Jesus' disciples had inquired about whom among them would be greatest in the kingdom of heaven, that he seized the opportunity to teach them about humility in general, while also specifically referring to his own humility, as the model of such humility. See the Scriptures below for more details:

> And he said: "Truly I tell you, unless you change and become like little children, you will never enter the kingdom of heaven. Therefore whoever takes the lowly position of this child is the greatest in the kingdom of heaven. And whoever welcomes one such child in my name welcomes me. (Matt 18:3–5, NIV)

Jesus, in the above-mentioned story, showed his disciples and indeed today's leaders that:

1. For one to be lifted up, they should first humble themselves.
2. Good leaders should associate with everyone, regardless of their social status.

Jesus Christ: The Model of Leadership

3. Leaders who humble themselves receive the respect and loyalty of their followers.

The leadership principle that Jesus was teaching his disciples in the above-mentioned story is that of:

- Humility.

It is those leaders who are humble and welcoming who stand the greatest chance of exerting a positive influence over their followers, who also want to be valued. These are the true leaders, because leadership is defined by an individual's ability to positively influence others towards desired directions, for without followership, we cannot talk about leadership.

Indeed, Jesus humbled himself by coming to earth in the form if sinful humanity, where he suffered many things, including being nailed on the cross; but once glorified, he was given the greatest name in heaven, on earth and under the earth!

Typical of the model of visionary leadership that Jesus was, he taught his disciples to embrace passion for the lost and to follow up on such in order to bring them back into the sheepfold, because God's will is that no one who has been called perishes. See the Scriptures below for more details:

> What do you think? If a man owns a hundred sheep, and one of them wanders away, will he not leave the ninety-nine on the hills and go to look for the one that wandered off? And if he finds it, truly I tell you, he is happier about that one sheep than about the ninety-nine that did not wander off. (Matt 18:12–13, NIV)

> In the same way your Father in heaven is not willing that any of these little ones should perish. (Matt 18:14, NIV)

The lessons that today's leaders can learn from the parable of the lost sheep are as follows:

1. Leaders should remain faithful to their calling and be good stewards of the sheep entrusted to their care.

2. The purpose or mission of leadership is, generally speaking, to ensure that those who have been called do not get lost, but remain in the "sheepfold."
3. Good leaders should ensure that all their subordinates work towards the realisation of organisational objectives, including actively following up on those failing to make the grade.

Taking a cue from Jesus, Paul reiterated the purpose of church leadership to the churches in Colossae and Thessalonica as follows:

> He is the one we proclaim, admonishing and teaching everyone with all wisdom, so that we may present everyone fully mature in Christ. (Col 1:28, NIV)

> For what is our hope, our joy, or crown in which we will glory in the presence of our Lord Jesus when he comes? Is it not you? Indeed you are our glory and joy. (1 Thess 2:19–20, NIV)

Through the above-mentioned parable, Jesus was imparting in his disciples the leadership principle of:

- Stewardship.

Leaders are called to be faithful stewards of the flocks (followers) entrusted to their care by ensuring they do not wander from the faith or depart from their core business in the circular world. They do this by following up those who would have backslidden in order to restore them back into the sheepfold or through the monitoring and evaluation of subordinates to ensure they do not depart from their core business.

Jesus-the model of visionary leadership-devoted much of his time to the teaching of his disciples and others. On one occasion when the Pharisees wanted to test his knowledge regarding the grounds for divorce, he showed them that God had initially designed marriage to be a permanent union, except in the case of infidelity. When the disciples had expressed their misgivings for marriage because it was meant to be a permanent union, Jesus

Jesus Christ: The Model of Leadership

showed them that there were some people who had the grace to choose celibacy in order for them to totally devote themselves to ministry. One such person was Paul. See the Scriptures below for more details:

> "I tell you that anyone who divorces his wife, except for sexual immorality, and marries another woman commits adultery." Then the disciples said to him, "If this is the situation between a husband and a wife, it is better not to marry." (Matt 19:9–10, NIV)

> For there are eunuchs who were born that way, and there are eunuchs who have been made eunuchs by others— and there are those who choose to live like eunuchs for the sake of the kingdom of heaven. The one who can accept this should accept it. (Matt 19:12, NIV)

The lessons to be learnt by today's leaders from Jesus' teachings cited above are as follows:

1. Leaders are called differently.
2. Leaders should not imitate other leaders' callings.
3. Leaders should embrace others with different callings.

Through the above-mentioned teaching, Jesus was imparting in his disciples the leadership principle of:

- Tolerance (of diversity).

Leaders who display tolerance for diversity also inspire their followers to do likewise. Tolerance by the leader also ensures that a harmonious work ethic pervades the entire organisation.

Jesus demonstrated visionary leadership, by remaining focussed on his vision as he and his disciples were leaving Jericho in regard to the two blind men who were calling for his attention, while the crowd was rebuking them. He went against the tide to display his abundant mercy and focus. See the Scriptures below for more details:

Template for Leadership

Two blind men were sitting by the roadside, and when they heard that Jesus was going by, they shouted, "Lord, son of David, have mercy on us!" The crowd rebuked them and told them to be quiet but they shouted all the louder, "Lord, son of David, have mercy on us!" Jesus stopped and called them, "What do you want me to do for you?" he asked. "Lord," they answered, "we want our sight." (Matt 20:30–33, NIV)

Jesus had compassion on them and then touched their eyes. Immediately they received their sight and followed him. (Matthew 20:34, NIV).

The lessons that leaders today can learn from the story of the two blind men mentioned above are as follows:

1. Leaders should also minister to the physical and or social needs of the people.
2. Leaders should be prepared to go against the tide in order to remain faithful to their calling.
3. Leaders should be prepared to always focus on their core business in spite of opposition.

The principles for today's leaders implicit in the story of the two blind men are the following:

- Compassion.
- Consistency.
- Strategic focus.

Compassionate and consistent leaders always gain the loyalty and respect of their followers. For Jesus Christ, driving out demons, healing the sick and restoring sight to the bind were all part of his core business that he never compromised on no matter what. Therefore all leaders who remain committed to their core business, no matter what, are more likely than not to realise their strategic goals.

Jesus Christ: The Model of Leadership

Jesus-the model of visionary leadership-used the fig tree incident detailed below to illustrate to his disciples that anything that may seem to be interfering with one's dream and or aspirations, no matter how big, can be overcome by faith. See the Scriptures below for more details:

> Early in the morning as Jesus was on his way back to the city, he was hungry. Seeing a fig tree by the roadside, he went up to it but found nothing on it except leaves. Then he said to it, "May you never bear fruit again!" Immediately the tree withered. When the disciples saw this they were amazed. "How did the fig tree wither so quickly?" they asked. (Matt 21:18–20, NIV)

> Jesus replied, "Truly if you have faith and do no doubt, not only can you do what was done to the fig tree but also you can say to this mountain, Go, throw yourself into the sea, and it will be done. If you believe you will receive whatever you ask for in prayer." (Matt 21:21–22, NIV)

The lessons that can be drawn by today's leaders from the fig tree incident are the following:

1. Any obstacle to one's dream, no matter how big can be removed by a prayer of faith as the cliché goes: 'Faith can move mountains.'
2. Faith is the key to answered prayer.
3. Leaders should therefore have an optimistic mind set in whatever they do; roll up their sleeves and get down to work and God will play his part.

The leadership principle implicit in the fig tree incident is that of:

- Faith/Optimism.

Therefore, in the face of any problem and or obstacle, leaders are encouraged to remain calm and hopeful that the Lord will answer their prayers and carry them through. A display of faith by the leader has the ripple effect of also inspiring faith in their followers.

Template for Leadership

Visionary leaders always show complementary leaders the way to go in order to fulfil their ultimate goal or vision. They also use teachable moments to impart strategic values and or practices.

Teachable moments are presenting situations or incidents that are used as springboards for appropriate teachings, as modelled by our Lord and Saviour Jesus Christ. And as the model of visionary leadership, Jesus Christ used the Pharisees' question regarding the greatest commandment to expose their hypocrisy concerning genuine love for others, by also teaching about the second most important commandment of loving your neighbour as yourself. See the Scriptures below for more details:

> Jesus replied, "Love the Lord your God with all your heart and with all your soul and with all your mind.' This is the first and greatest commandment. And the second is like it: 'Love your neighbour as yourself.' Deut 6:5; Lev 19:18. (Matt 22:37–39, NIV)

> Then Jesus said to the crowds and to his disciples: "The teachers of the law and the Pharisees sit in Moses' seat. So you must be careful to do everything they tell you. But do not do what they do for they do not practice what they preach." (Matt 23:1–3, NIV)

The lessons that can be learnt by leaders today, from the above-mentioned story are the following:

1. Top leaders should ensure that complementary leaders remain faithful to their mandate, through appropriate coaching and or relevant teachings.
2. Leaders should identify and use teachable moments with their followers.
3. Church leaders should teach their followers to have total devotion for God.
4. Church leaders should encourage their followers to genuinely love one another.
5. Leaders should practice what they preach.

Jesus Christ: The Model of Leadership

The leadership principles implicit in Jesus' teachings cited above are the following:

- Strategic focus.
- Faithfulness.
- Integrity.

Leaders with a strategic focus never lose focus of the bigger picture by shunning practices and values that do not feed into the existing vision. Faithfulness is underlined by the fact that if one truly loves God with all their heart and with all their soul and with all their mind, they steer clear of duplicity and obey all his commandments, including loving one's neighbour as themselves. They also do what they preach, unlike the Pharisees whose work ethic could be characterised by the cliché that goes: "Do as I say and not as I do."

Faithful leaders are men and women of integrity as they earn for themselves the respect and honour of their followers.

Leaders who do not remain faithful to their calling risk stiffer punishment than ordinary church members as the Scripture on the teachers of the law cited below alludes to:

> These men will be punished most severely. (Luke 20:47b, NIV)

This standard also applies to business leaders, who fail to stick to their core business. They risk dismissal much more than junior employees, who in most cases, get away with a mere reprimand.

Jesus Christ, as the model of visionary leadership, taught his disciples the strategic principles or values of diligence, faithfulness and good stewardship by relating the parable of the bags of gold. See the Scriptures below for further details:

> To one he gave five bags of gold, to another two bags and to another one bag. Each according to his ability." (Matt 25:15, NIV)

> The man who had received five bags of gold brought the other five, 'Master,' he said, 'you entrusted me with five

Template for Leadership

bags of gold. See, I have gained five more.' His master replied, 'Well done, good and faithful servant! You have been faithful with a few things. I will put you in charge of many things.' (Matt 25:20–21a, NIV)

The man with two bags of gold also came. 'Master,' he said, 'you entrusted me with two bags of gold. See I have gained two more.' His master replied, "Well done good and faithful servant! You have been faithful with a few things; I will put you in charge of many things." (Matt 25:22–23a, NIV)

Then the one who had received one bag of gold came. 'Master,' he said, 'I knew you are a hard man, harvesting where you did not sow and gathering where you have not scattered seed. So I was afraid and went out and hid your gold in the ground. See, here is what belongs to you' . . ."So take the bag of gold from him and give to the one who has ten bags. For whoever has will be given more and they will have in abundance. Whoever does not have even what they have will be taken from them. And throw that worthless servant outside, into the darkness where there will be weeping and gnashing of teeth." (Matt 25:28–30, NIV)

The parable of the bags of gold is relevant to leadership because it is usually managers or people in leadership positions who are entrusted with investment decisions unlike shop floor workers, who are assigned day-to-day operational duties.

The lessons that can be drawn by today's leaders from the parable of the bags of gold are as follows:

1. God gives people unique anointing and or competencies.
2. God judges people on the basis of their gifts.
3. God expects leaders to be good stewards of the resources and or capabilities at their disposal.
4. God will reward or punish leaders depending on whether or not they have been faithful to their calling.

Jesus Christ: The Model of Leadership

5. God will reward or punish leaders depending on their diligence or lack thereof in the area of their gifting.

Please note that by competences, we are referring to the things an individual does very well compared with others; commonly known as 'talents.'

Three leadership principles emanating from the parable of the bags of gold are the following:

- Diligence.
- Faithfulness.
- Stewardship (of God-given resources and or capabilities).

Leaders who are diligent; who serve faithfully and are good stewards of their God-given resources and or capabilities receive the favour and loyalty of their followers, enabling the former to positively influence the latter along desired directions.

In the business world, a manager or leader who fails to deploy available resources into the generation of more wealth and also departs from their prescribed core business is more likely than not to get punished or removed from their position. This shows that diligence, faithfulness and good stewardship are indeed vital for anyone who wants to take their leadership seriously.

On the other hand, business leaders who are diligent; are faithful to their core business and who deploy available resources towards the creation of more wealth get rewarded or promoted.

Our Lord and Savior, Jesus Christ is the perfect example of sacrificial leadership in that he endured slander, mockery, and beatings before being crucified on the cross without protesting, because he knew that this is what it would take to save mankind from perishing. See the Scripture below on Jesus' selfless demeanour:

> He was oppressed and afflicted, yet he did not open his mouth; like a lamb to the slaughter, and as a sheep before its shearers is silent, so he did not open his mouth. (Isa 53:7, NIV)

Template for Leadership

The lessons to be learnt by today's leaders from Jesus' display of sacrificial leadership cited above are as follows:

1. Leaders should be steadfast or have a thick skin and be prepared to suffer persecution and or opposition; if this is what it takes to accomplish their vision.
2. Leaders should exercise self-control and restraint and not be involved in shouting matches with those abusing them.

The principles implicit in Jesus' mind-set cited above are the following:

- Selflessness.
- Commitment.
- Steadfastness.
- Restraint.

Selflessness in meeting the needs of others, results in the leader gaining the favour of his/her followers, while commitment to a cause, and steadfastness no matter what, motivates followers to emulate their leaders.

Restraint earns leaders the respect and admiration of their followers, making the former become more acceptable to the latter. Leader acceptability will then galvanise the cooperation of followers, making the leaders more influential with them in the long term.

As the epitome of sacrificial leadership, Jesus laid down his life for our salvation:

> Greater love has no one than this: to lay down one's life for one's friends. (John 15:14, NIV)

The lessons that today's leaders can learn from Jesus' example are as follows:

1. Leaders should prioritise the needs of others ahead of their own comfort.
2. Leaders should avail their time and resources to meet the needs of others.

Jesus Christ: The Model of Leadership

The leadership principles implicit in Jesus' sacrificial leadership are the following:

- Selflessness.
- Responsiveness.
- Good stewardship.

The above-mentioned virtues serve to endear leaders to their followers and the wider society, just as Jesus Christ's global acceptability and impact on the world stage has been unrivalled and unmatched.

Sacrificial leadership could be expressed like in the scenarios described below:

Scenario 1

In the face of a sudden increase in the price of basic commodities, management could consider foregoing or revising their holiday packages, to accommodate a deserving-albeit modest—pay rise for their employees.

Scenario 2

A couple that has just had a nasty fight that knocks at the pastor's door at 9 o'clock at night seeking counselling, should not be turned away and advised to come back at a more convenient time for the latter. Rather, the pastor should go out of his/her way to accommodate the couple's needs. If the pastor accommodates the couple, he/she gains the respect and admiration of the entire church. If on the other hand, they choose to go by the rule book, they risk attracting the censure of the entire church.

Template for Leadership

Scenario 3

A church deacon is making preparations to give his family a treat by taking them to an exclusive restaurant for dinner, when suddenly a poor widow shows up to ask for money for her children's school fees.

Faced by such a dilemma, what should the deacon do? Well, your guess is as good as mine: the good deacon should call off the dinner and help out the poor lady!

Having witnessed the love shown by the deacon, many other people may be led to Christ, showing that good leaders have a positive influence on society. In any case:

> Religion which God our Father accepts as pure and faultless is this: to look after orphans and widows in their distress and to keep .one from being polluted by the world. (Jas 1: 27, NIV)

Our Lord and Savior, Jesus Christ was the perfect example of selflessness and meeting the needs of others ahead of his own: a perfect example of sacrificial and or shepherd leadership. See the Scripture below for your motivation:

> I am the good shepherd. The good shepherd lays down his life for the sheep. (John 10:11, NIV)

In the above-cited Scripture, Jesus Christ was referring to his coming down to earth to be sacrificed on the cross for the sake of our salvation, while foregoing the majesty of heaven.

The lessons for today's leaders emanating from Jesus' sacrificial leadership cited above are as follows:

1. Leaders should strive to meet the needs of others ahead of their own.
2. Leaders should own up to the mistakes of their followers, even at the risk to their own safety or dignity as a demonstration of sacrificial leadership.

The leadership principles implicit in the above-cited Scripture on Jesus' sacrificial leadership are the following:

Jesus Christ: The Model of Leadership

- Responsiveness.
- Selflessness.

Leaders who respond to the needs of others-even to the extent of putting their own at stake-display selflessness and become more likely to receive the loyalty of their followers who then become amenable to the former's direction in future endeavours.

Our Lord and Saviour, Jesus Christ—as the model leader-was always ready to meet people's needs and to also give unconditional love, as demonstrated by his interaction with the man suffering from leprosy in a in a display of sacrificial leadership. See the Scripture below for more details:

> When Jesus came down from the mountainside, large crowds followed him. A man with leprosy came and knelt before him and said, "Lord if you are willing, you can make me clean." Jesus reached out his hand and touched the man." "I am willing," he said, "Be clean!" (Matthew 8:1–3, NIV)

In those days, people with leprosy were actually shunned—to the extent of being quarantined—because the other people who had no leprosy were afraid to contract the disease. But in spite of conventional wisdom, Jesus reached out and touched him, before commanding his healing, in a show of unconditional love and responsiveness to the man's needs. Indeed this was a perfect example of sacrificial leadership.

Two lessons which leaders today can learn from Jesus' example are as follows:

1. Leaders should always be willing to meet the needs of others (their followers and the wider society).
2. Leaders should embrace everyone, regardless of their physical and or social condition.

By so doing, leaders stand to gain the favour and loyalty of their followers, because without 'followership' there is no leadership.

Template for Leadership

The leadership principles inherent in Jesus' dealings with the leprous man are the following:

- Responsiveness.
- Non-discrimination.

Leaders who do not discriminate against others, regardless of their physical and or material condition and who also respond to people's pressing needs, tend to be more acceptable to their followers.

Jesus also used his interaction with the rich young man to impart the essence or significance of sacrificial leadership to his disciples. This can also be applied to all success-oriented leaders. The rich young man had come to Jesus to inquire about what good thing he had not yet done that was needed for him to enter the kingdom of God. Jesus mentioned the commandments, to which the young man indicated he had kept them all. But when Jesus told the young men to go and sell all his possessions and follow him, the latter went away dejected. The following passage of Scripture is very instructive in that regard:

> Just then a man came up to Jesus and asked, "Teacher, what good thing must I do to get eternal life?". . . "All these I have kept," the young man said. "What do I still lack?" Jesus answered, "If you want to be perfect, go, sell your possessions and give to the poor, and you will have treasure in heaven. Then come follow me." When the young man heard this, he went away sad because he had great wealth. (Matt 19:16; 20, 21–22, NIV)

After the above-mentioned incident, Jesus assured his disciples that because they had sacrificed everything to follow him; they would sit on twelve thrones, judging the twelve tribes of Israel in heaven, while others who had also left everything for the sake of the gospel would receive eternal life. See the Scriptures below for more details:

> Jesus said to them, "Truly I tell you, at the renewal of all things, when the Son of Man sits on his glorious throne, you who have followed me will also sit on

Jesus Christ: The Model of Leadership

twelve thrones, judging the twelve tribes of Israel. And everyone who has left houses or brothers or sisters or father or mother or wife or children for my sake will receive a hundred times as much and will inherit eternal life." (Matt 19:28–29, NIV)

The lessons for leaders today from the above-mentioned interactions are as follows:

1. No one is perfect; therefore leaders should never be self-conceited.
2. Good leadership is never a destination, but a continual process.
3. Reward comes only `after sacrifice.

The principles that the above-mentioned story imparts to today's leaders are the following:

- Humility.
- Commitment.
- Non-complacence.

Humility and commitment by leaders not only earns them acceptance and admiration from followers, but also has the positive ripple effect of inspiring the same values in the latter. It should also be noted that a leader who is complacent is setting him/herself for failure, since a "have arrived" mentality has no place in leadership.

When Jesus sent out his twelve disciples, he warned them of potential persecution-an apt reminder of the fact that leadership is inherently sacrificial. See the Scripture below for more details on this subject:

> I am sending you out like sheep among the wolves . . . Be on your guard: you will be handed over to the local councils and be flogged in the synagogues. (Matt 10:16a; 17, NIV)

Jesus' warning to the disciples cited above, shows that leadership is not a stroll in the park, but is accompanied by trials and temptations that call for perseverance, as he himself was the perfect example of perseverance, as alluded to by the Scripture below:

Template for Leadership

And let us run with perseverance the race marked out for us, fixing our eyes on Jesus, the pioneer and perfector of our faith. For the joy before him, he endured the cross and sat down at the right hand of God. (Heb 12:1b–2, NIV)

Indeed Paul also reminds Timothy-a complementary leader- of the inevitability of persecution when he remarked in the Scripture below that:

In fact everyone who wants to live a godly life in Christ Jesus will be persecuted. (2 Tim 3:12, NIV)

Of course Paul's sentiments mentioned above do not exclude today's leaders!

Persecution has always been inevitable for leaders who challenged dominant traditions while seeking to advance alternative views since time immemorial. Since Jesus' time onwards, countless leaders have faced persecution-including martyrdom-for abandoning Judaism and other forms of traditional worship in favour of Christianity. Leaders are often targeted because they usually exert a great deal of influence over large numbers of people.

The lessons to be drawn by today's leaders from the above-quoted Scriptures are as follows:

1. Persecution or opposition in leadership is inevitable.
2. Leaders should persevere in the face of persecution because they will be rewarded for their unwavering commitment.
3. The greater the persecution the greater the reward, as they say in business: "high risk high return."

The leadership principles implicit in Jesus' teachings, cited above, for leaders today, are as follows:

- Commitment.
- Steadfastness.

Leaders are therefore encouraged to embrace the virtues of commitment and steadfastness to God's work no matter what, as the Scripture below aptly encourages:

Jesus Christ: The Model of Leadership

Whoever finds their life will lose it, and whoever loses their life for my sake will find it. (Luke 10:39, NIV)

In fact, even for non-church leaders, persecution is inevitable, since they are also held accountable should anything go wrong in their organisations, while in most instances they are not acknowledged for the good that they would have done.

Leaders, who show total commitment to their calling and do not waver in spite of persecution, get the admiration of their followers, who also become motivated to do likewise. Again commitment and steadfastness are indeed necessary for the accomplishment of a leader's vision.

Jesus-as the embodiment of sacrificial leadership-had on one occasion to forego his quiet time of prayer and meditation after the beheading of John the Baptist, in order to attend to people's physical needs. See the Scripture below for further details:

> When Jesus heard what had happened, he withdrew privately by boat to a solitary place. Hearing of this, the crowds followed him on foot from the towns. When Jesus landed and saw a large crowd, he had compassion on them and healed their sick. (Matt 14:13-14, NIV)

The lessons to be learnt from the above-mentioned incident by today's leaders are as follows:

1. Leaders should always be ready to meet people's needs even if this means foregoing their own comfort or priorities.
2. Leaders should always be prepared to change their programmes in order to attend to people's urgent needs.
3. Leaders should be compassionate.

The leadership principles implicit in Jesus' actions cited above are the following:

- Compassion.
- Flexibility.
- Responsiveness.

Template for Leadership

Compassion, responsiveness to people's needs and flexibility in a leader's approach make them the darling of their followers and this elicits the followers' loyalty and cooperation with the leader.

At Caesarea Philippi, Jesus used Peter's rebuke as a teachable moment to motivate his disciples to embrace sacrificial leadership- even to the point of death-in order to receive a befitting reward since there is no gain without pain. Again, the bigger the sacrifice, the bigger the reward! See the Scriptures below for more details:

> From that time on Jesus began to explain to his disciples that he must go to Jerusalem and suffer many things at the hands of the elders, the chief priests and teachers of the law, and that he must be killed and on the third day be raised to life. (Matt 16:21, NIV)
>
> Peter took him aside and began to rebuke him. "Never, Lord!" he said. "This shall never happen to you!"(Matt 16:22, NIV)
>
> Then Jesus said to his disciples, "Whoever wants to be my disciple must deny themselves and take up their cross and follow me. For whoever wants to save their life will lose it, but whoever loses their life for my sake will find it . . . For the Son of Man is going to come in his Father's glory with his angels, and then he will reward each person according to what they have done." (Matt 16:24–25; 27, NIV)

Therefore, leaders who want to receive a great reward must be prepared to put their head on the chopping block!

The lessons for today's leaders from the above-mentioned story are as follows:

1. Leadership involves sacrifice.
2. The bigger the sacrifice, the bigger the reward.

Jesus used the Caesarea Philippi incident as a teachable moment to impart to his disciples the leadership principle of:

- Commitment.

Jesus Christ: The Model of Leadership

If a leader is totally committed to his calling, no matter what, they gain the respect and loyalty of their followers, and this ensures that leaders always achieve their goals.

Finally, our Lord and Saviour, Jesus Christ demonstrated the highest level of sacrificial leadership by embracing the ultimate price for our redemption on Calvary in a show of total commitment and selflessness in pursuit of his vision or assignment. The Scriptures below amply reflect Jesus' total commitment and selflessness:

> Going a little further he fell with his face to the ground and prayed, "My Father, if it is possible, may this cup be taken from me. Yet not as I will, but as you will."(Matt 26:39, NIV)

> He went away a second time and prayed, "My Father, if it not possible for this cup to be taken away from me unless I drink it, may your will be done."(Matt 26:42, NIV)

The lessons that leaders can draw from Jesus' example cited above are the following:

1. Leaders should have total commitment to their vision.
2. Leaders should persevere no matter what, in order to accomplish their vision.
3. Leaders need to pursue a cause that is greater than themselves in order to inspire others.

The leadership principles implicit in Jesus' example cited above are the following:

- Commitment.
- Perseverance.
- Altruism.

Leaders, who display total commitment to their vision even to the point of death, and persevere in the face of seemingly insurmountable adversity, gain the admiration of their followers; while they also earn followership (buy-in) for their cause. Leaders who

Template for Leadership

follow Jesus Christ's example of self-sacrifice and altruism inspire others in unimaginable ways. For instance, Christianity is the world's biggest religion largely because of Jesus' sacrificial leadership.

Our Lord and Saviour, Jesus Christ was the perfect example of perseverance and or consistency in that though he was tempted, persecuted and crucified on the cross for the sake of our salvation, he endured till the end, thereby displaying exemplary leadership.

Jesus' perseverance in the face of intense suffering, has therefore, made him the model empathiser.

See the Scriptures below on Jesus' example of perseverance that earned him the position of chief empathiser:

> For we do not have a high priest who is unable to empathize with our weaknesses, but we have one who has been tempted in every way, just as we are-yet he did not sin. (Heb 4:15, NIV)

In another place, the Bible has this to say about Jesus' perseverance:

> He was oppressed and afflicted, yet he did not open his mouth; like a lamb to the slaughter, and as a sheep before its shearers is silent, so he did not open his mouth. (Isa 53:7, NIV)

The lessons to be leant by today's leaders from Jesus' exemplary leadership are as follows:

1. Good leaders should be consistent and not waver, whatever the situation.

2. Good leaders should be empathetic by always appreciating the needs, feelings and viewpoints of others.

3. Leaders should be models of perseverance in the face of adversity; rather than crying with their followers.

4. Leaders should inspire hope where there is no hope, because, as the Psalmist says:

> Weeping may stay for the night, but rejoicing comes in the morning. (Psalm 30:5b, NIV)

Jesus Christ: The Model of Leadership

Five leadership principles that emerge from Jesus' exemplary leadership, cited above, are the following:

- Commitment.
- Perseverance.
- Empathy.
- Consistency.
- Leadership.

It is through commitment, perseverance and empathy that leaders gain the trust and confidence of others, resulting in them having a positive influence on their followers. Leaders, who display consistency by persevering in the face of adversity, also inspire their followers to do the same. And this also makes the followers more amenable to the leader's direction in the future, which is the hallmark of effective leadership.

Our Lord and Saviour, Jesus Christ, as the model of exemplary leadership, taught his disciples and demonstrated civil obedience when he sent Peter to catch a fish in order to retrieve the money with which to pay his and Peter's temple tax, although he was the Son of God-the owner of that temple-as the children of the kings of this world are exempt from the payment of tax.

Jesus did this to demonstrate to his disciples that a leader leads by example and that leaders are also peacemakers. See the Scripture below for more details:

> But so that we may not cause offense, go to the lake and throw out your line. Take the first fish you catch; open its mouth and you will find a four-drachma coin. Take it and give it to them for my tax and yours. (Matt 17:27, NIV)

The lessons to be learnt from Jesus' actions in the above-mentioned story are as follows:

1. Leaders should lead by example.
2. Church leaders should also pay their tithes.

Template for Leadership

3. Leaders should be peacemakers who should bend backwards for the sake of peace.

Jesus, in the above-mentioned story, illustrated two leadership principles:

- Credibility.
- Faithfulness.

Faithful leaders lead by example in such areas as tithing and payment of taxes, which in turn motivates their followers to do the same. By so doing, they also increase their credibility as they meet their civil obligations so as not disrupt established social orders.

Jesus also used the imperial tax incident to demonstrate exemplary leadership to his disciples and others by encouraging people to fulfil their legal obligations by paying the imperial tax to Caesar, as the Pharisees and Herodians tried to lay a trap against him. See the Scripture below for more details:

> "Tell us then, what is your opinion? Is it right to pay the imperial tax to Caesar or not?" But Jesus aware of their evil intent, said, "You hypocrites, why are you trying to trap me? Show me the coin used for paying the tax." They brought him a denarius and he asked them, "Whose image is this? And whose inscription?" "Caesar's," they replied. Then he said to them, "So give to Caesar what is Caesar's, and to God, what is God's." (Matt 22:17–21, NIV)

Today's leaders can learn from the imperial tax story the following lessons:

1. Leaders should be beyond reproach.
2. Leaders should fulfil all their obligations.
3. Leaders should submit to civil authorities, so they may work in peace without let or hindrance.
4. Leaders should be exemplary.

The leadership principle that can be borrowed from the above-mentioned story is that of:

Jesus Christ: The Model of Leadership

- Integrity.

Leaders with integrity have credibility with their followers and are therefore more likely than not to gain the respect and loyalty of the latter.

Our Lord and Saviour, Jesus Christ was also the perfect example and model of complementary leadership by choosing the twelve apostles to work with and complement him. See the Scripture below on this subject:

> One of those days Jesus went out to a mountainside to pray and spent the night praying to God. When morning came, he called his disciples to him and chose twelve of them, whom he also designated as apostles. (Luke 6:12–13, NIV)

The lessons to be learnt by today's leaders from the choosing of the twelve apostles are as follows:

1. Shared leadership creates synergies or complementarity.
2. Leadership is a shared enterprise.

The leadership principles implicit in Jesus' choosing of the twelve disciples are the following:

- Building of synergies.
- Participation.

Involvement of others in decision-making creates a sense of ownership and acceptability of all decisions by the entire leadership team. The building of synergy is likely to result in more robust decisions and programmes for any organisation.

4

The Call to Leadership
The Case of Moses

To be an effective church or ministry leader, you should have been called to do so. If one hasn't been sent by God, they should never venture into ministry, for they would be lacking the accompanying anointing. They also labour in vain as they won't receive any reward for their work, since they would not have been sent. In fact if one were to pretend to have been called, they stand to fail miserably for lack of a guiding vision and the accompanying anointing.

Consider Moses' call and vision to deliver the children of Israel from Egyptian slavery to the Promised Land:

> The LORD said, "I have indeed seen the misery of my people in Egypt. I have heard them crying out because of their slave drivers, and I am concerned about their suffering. So I have come down to rescue them from the hand of the Egyptians and to bring them up out of that land into a good and spacious land, a land flowing with milk and honey ... So now, go. I am sending you to Pharaoh to bring my people the Israelites out of Egypt." (Exod 3:7–8a; 10, NIV)

The Call to Leadership: The Case of Moses

So, if one has been called by God, they are also given the vision or assignment to go with that call. Moses' vision was to deliver the children of Israel from Egyptian slavery.

If one has been called by God to ministry, God will also stand by them to see their work through, whatever the circumstances. This was shown by God's dialogue with Moses, after the latter had expressed lack of confidence in his own ability to deliver the Israelites out of Pharaoh's strong hand. See the dialogue cited below for your encouragement:

> But Moses said to God, "Who am I that I should go to Pharaoh and bring the Israelites out of Egypt?" And God said, "I will be with you." (Exod 3:11–12a, NIV)

The above-cited dialogue shows that if one has been called to leadership, they should not stand on their own ability as God himself would be their enabler.

Where one has been called by God, they also receive the accompanying favor (influence to lead) as well as the required strategies for accomplishing the task. See God's assurance to Moses in the Scripture cited below:

> The elders of Israel will listen to you. Then you and the elders are to go to the king of Egypt and say to him, 'The LORD, the God of the Hebrews, has met with us. Let us take a three day journey into the wilderness to offer sacrifices to the LORD our God.' But I know that the king of Egypt will not let you go unless a mighty hand compels him. So I will stretch out my hand and strike the Egyptians with all the wonders that I will perform among them. After that, he will let you go. (Exod 3:18–20, NIV)

God reveals any likely opposition to be encountered in one's mission and also gives assurance for the success of that mission beforehand, since he declares the end from the beginning, as an omniscient God (Isaiah 46:10). In any case, God's purpose will always prevail (Proverbs 21:30).

The lessons to be learnt by today's leaders from Moses' call are as follows:

Template for Leadership

1. For one to do God's work, they need to have been called.
2. The call to leadership comes with a clear and specific vision or assignment.
3. Leaders do not go forth on their own strength, because God will always be their strength.

The leadership principles implicit in the call of Moses are the following:

- Responsiveness.
- Clarity of vision.

If one has been called by God they should respond to the call because God will always anoint them for the work ahead and stand by them. They should also articulate a clear and worthwhile vision for ease of buy-in by their followers. In Moses' case the vision was that of liberation and it resonated well with the Israelites' aspirations of freedom from Egyptian slavery.

The modus operandi of Moses and Aaron is a practical example of complementary leadership, since the call to leadership is not a loner's journey. Visionary leaders should present the vision while complimentary leaders support the vision and "run with it" i.e. champion it and translate it into action.

While visionary leaders should clearly articulate their God-given vision for his work, complimentary leaders should ensure its execution. Of course, in addition to articulating the vision, visionary leaders are responsible for monitoring and evaluation to ensure alignment of implementation with the original vision.

See the Scripture below on the complementarity that existed between Moses and Aaron:

> Moses said to the LORD, "Pardon your servant LORD. I have never been eloquent, neither in the past nor since you have spoken to your servant. I am slow of speech and tongue.". . . But Moses said, "Pardon your servant, LORD. Please send someone else.". . . Then the LORD's anger burned against Moses and he said, "What about your brother, Aaron the Levite? I know he can speak well

The Call to Leadership: The Case of Moses

> ... He will speak to the people for you, and it will be as if he were your mouth and as if you were God to him."
> (Exod 4:10; 13–14, 16, NIV)

God's anger burned against Moses, probably because the latter had been too quick to acknowledge his deficiencies and declined being sent to deliver the Israelites from Pharaoh's strong hand as if it all depended on his own ability. It also appeared as if Moses wanted to pre-empt God's plan.

Unbeknown to Moses, God had already devised a way out by making Aaron available to complement him as he added in reference to Aaron:

> He is already on his way to meet you, and he will be glad to see you. (Exod 4:14b, NIV)

The story of Moses and Aaron is an illustration of the fact that if one has been called to church or ministry leadership, God will always raise others to complement them.

Therefore, if one has a calling for ministry, they should take heart; God will never send them alone!

The lessons today's leaders should learn from Moses' and Aaron's example are as follows:

1. Leadership is a shared enterprise.
2. Leaders complement each other.
3. Visionary leaders should clearly articulate the vision to others.
4. Complementary leaders should meticulously implement the given vision.

The principles underpinning Moses' and Aaron's work ethic are the following:

- Cooperation.
- Building synergies.

Cooperation among leaders ensures success in whatever they set out to do, as the following cliché aptly implies:

'United we stand; divided we fall.'

Template for Leadership

Indeed everything stands and falls on unity of purpose-or lack of it-among the leaders. And as the leaders cooperate, they build synergies through a higher probability of non-overlapping weaknesses.

Aaron's preparedness to play a subservient role to that of Moses, his younger brother, is indeed a display of humility, on his part.

The leadership lessons to be learnt from Aaron's example are as follows:

1. Complementary leaders—as indeed all leaders-should be humble.
2. Complementary leaders should run with the vision articulated by visionary leaders.

Aaron's demeanour serves to inspire today's leaders to embrace the principles of:

- Humility.
- Faithfulness.
- Service.

Complementary leaders who are humble, subservient to their visionary leader and willing to serve faithfully in line with their calling, contribute positively to the achievement of the existing vision.

The story of Moses and the Israelites is an illustration of how God can lead a church or ministry, as long as the one, who is called to be the overall leader, remains faithful to the vision of their call, and open to the leading of the Holy Spirit. See the Scriptures below for further enlightenment:

> By day the LORD went ahead of them in a pillar of cloud, to guide them on their way and by night in a pillar of fire to give them light so that they could travel by day or night. (Exod 13:24, NIV)

> In all the travels of the Israelites, whenever the cloud lifted from above the tabernacle, they would set out; but

The Call to Leadership: The Case of Moses

if the cloud did not lift, they did no set out until the day it lifted. (Exod 40:36–37, NIV)

The lessons that today's leaders could learn from Moses' leadership are as follows:

1. Church leaders should remain sensitive to the leading of the Holy Spirit.
2. Leaders in the circular world should always be guided by their strategic goals and operational mandates.

The leadership principle implicit in the above-cited story is that of:

- Submissiveness.

Church or ministry leaders who submit to the leading of the Holy Spirit succeed in achieving their vision because the Holy Spirit is omniscient. Circular leaders who meticulously stick to their operational mandates also achieve their strategic goals.

Moses, in line with exemplary leadership, showed that good leadership does not consist of crying with the followers, but in inspiring hope and encouragement, in the face of adversity. See the Scriptures below for your inspiration:

> As Pharaoh approached, the Israelites looked up, and there were the Egyptians marching after them. They were terrified and cried out to the LORD. They said to Moses, "Was it because there were no graves in Egypt that you brought us to the dessert to die? What have you done to us by bringing us out of Egypt?" (Exod 14:10–11, NIV)

> Moses answered the people, "Do not be afraid, stand firm and you will see the deliverance the LORD will bring you today. The Egyptians you see today you will never see again. The LORD will fight for you: you need only to be still." (Exod 14:13–14, NIV)

The lessons that today's leaders can learn from the above-mentioned story of Moses and the Israelites are as follows:

Template for Leadership

1. A good leader always encourages others and urges them on in the face of adversity.
2. A good leader should be tenacious or resolute in the face of opposition.

The leadership principle displayed by Moses in the face of the approaching Egyptians is that of:

- Steadfastness/perseverance.

Steadfastness and or perseverance will always lead to the achievement of a leader's goals as it often galvanises the whole team and urges them on. If the leader throws their hands up in despair or cries with his/her followers in the face of challenges, the entire team gets discouraged, leading to failure in the achievement of set goals.

In line with sacrificial leadership, Moses was prepared to put his head on the chopping block, for the sake of his flock as shown by his intercession for the Israelites at Mount Sinai when God wanted to wipe them out after they had made and worshipped a golden calf.

When it seemed Moses wouldn't be coming down from Mount Sinai-where he had gone to receive God's commandments and had been up there for a long time-the Israelites asked Aaron to make them gods that would direct them on their way; whereupon the latter asked for gold earrings from the women, boys and girls and made them an idol in the form of a calf.

After the above-mentioned incident, God's anger burned against the Israelites and he threatened to destroy them and instead make Moses into a great nation. However, Moses sacrificially interceded for them, denying the favor of being made into a great nation himself. He even went as far as offering to be blotted from the book of life, if this is what it would take to spare the Israelites from destruction. See the Scriptures below for further details:

> "I have seen these people," the LORD said to Moses, "they are a stiff-necked people. Now leave me alone so that my anger may burn against them and that I may destroy them. Then I will make you into a great nation." (Exod 32:9–10, NIV)

The Call to Leadership: The Case of Moses

> But Moses sought the favor of the Lord his God. "LORD," he said, "Why should your anger burn against your people, whom you brought out of Egypt with great power and a mighty hand? Why should the Egyptians say, "It was with evil intent that he brought them out to kill them in the mountains and to wipe them off the face of the earth? Turn from your fierce anger, relent and do not bring disaster on your people. Remember your servants Abraham, Isaac and Israel by whom you swore by your own self: 'I will make your descendants as numerous as the stars in the sky and I will give your descendants all this land I have promised them, and it will be their inheritance forever.' (Exod 32:11–13, NIV)

> So Moses went back to the LORD and said, "Oh, what a great sin these people have committed! They have made themselves gods of gold. But now, please forgive their sin-but if not, then blot me out of the book you have written. " (Exod 32:31–32, NIV)

> Then the LORD relented and did not bring on his people the disaster he had threatened. (Exodus 32:14, NIV)

Although the Lord had promised to make Moses into a great nation if he destroyed the Israelites, Moses did not seek his own personal glory, but was prepared to put his own head on the chopping block for the benefit of others. Moses' sacrificial attitude serves to reflect that of Jesus Christ, making him a topology of Jesus; who would later be sacrificed and die on the cross so that humanity would be spared from death and eternal condemnation, as captured by the Scripture cited below:

> He forgave us all our sins, having cancelled the charge of our legal indebtedness, which stood against us and condemned us; he has taken it away nailing it to the cross. (Col 2:13b–14, NIV)

Moses' example of sacrificial leadership has the following implications for today's leaders:

Template for Leadership

1. Leaders should be sacrificial, selfless and seek the benefit of others ahead of their own.
2. Church or ministry leaders should also be great intercessors.
3. Where complaints are raised by clients and or customers, the leader should own up, apologise and rectify the problem without necessarily exposing the concerned employees to further public humiliation and ridicule.

The leadership principle displayed by Moses' at Mount Sinai is that of:

- Selflessness.

If God reveals sin in the church, sacrificial leaders should own up and intercede for the church for God's forgiveness, instead of being guided by the cliché:

'Each man for himself and God for us all!'

Sacrificial leaders give their time and forego their comfort, by going into prayer and fasting, in order to intercede for the sins of the church or of their followers.

Complementary leadership was displayed at Rephidim where the Israelites defeated the Amalekites. It took the cooperation of four leaders to defeat them when they had attacked Israel. Joshua and his men engaged in direct combat, while Moses, Aaron, and Hur went up the hill to hold up the staff of God.

As long as Moses held up his hands, the Israelites prevailed but whenever he lowered his hands, the Amalekites were winning. However, when Moses grew weary, it took the cooperation of Aaron and Hur to turn the tide in the favor of the Israelites. See the Scripture below on this subject:

> When Moses' hands grew tired, they took a stone and put it under him and he sat on it. Aaron and Hur held his hands up-one on one side, one on the other-so that his hands remained steady till sunset. So Joshua overcame the Amalekite army with the sword. (Exodus 17:12–13, NIV)

The Call to Leadership: The Case of Moses

The lessons that today's leaders can learn from the Rephidim battle are as follows:

1. To achieve any goal, leaders need to have unity of purpose.
2. Leadership is a shared enterprise.

The leadership principles implicit in the Rephidim encounter, are the following:

- Unity.
- Cooperation.

As the cliché goes: United we stand, divided we fall; so it is with leadership! Cooperation or teamwork among leaders augurs well for success while opposition and conflict among them results in lack of focus and failure in whatever leaders set out to do.

Jethro's advice to Moses cited below, shows that leadership should always be shared in order to protect the overall leader from experiencing burnout. Jethro, after observing Moses hearing people's cases, advised the latter, to appoint others who would preside as judges over the people and only bring him the difficult cases. Through his advice, Jethro was in actual fact urging Moses to embrace complementary leadership .See the Scriptures below for further details:

> Moses' father-in-law replied, "What you are doing is not good. You and these people who come to you will only wear yourselves out. The work is too heavy for you; you cannot handle it alone." (Exod 18:17–18, NIV)

> But select men from all the people-men who fear God, trustworthy men who hate dishonest gain-and appoint them as officials over thousands, hundreds, fifties and tens. Let them sit as judges for the people at all times, but have them bring every difficult case to you; the simple cases they can decide themselves. That will make your load lighter, because they will share it with you. (Exod 18:21–22, NIV)

Template for Leadership

The lessons to be learnt by today's leaders from Jethro's advice to Moses are as follows:

1. Overall leaders should share the burden of leadership with complementary leaders in order to avoid burnout.
2. When God calls someone to church or ministry leadership, he never sends them alone, but makes others available to complement them.
3. Top organisational leaders should incorporate others in decision-making.

The leadership principles implicit in Jethro's advice to Moses are the following:

- Participation.
- Joint decision-making.
- Delegation.

To avoid burnout, leaders should share tasks and decision-making with others. Complementary leaders could be assigned simpler tasks such as administrative duties; baptism, children's and youth ministries, while overall leaders do the main preaching, counselling, deliverance and overall church direction.

The story of Moses is a typology of redemption wherein Moses stands for Jesus and Pharaoh, Satan. Moses' vision to deliver the Israelites from Egyptian oppression is a picture of what was to come: Jesus' redemption of mankind from satanic oppression. Similarly, anyone who has been called to church leadership is expected to share with Jesus the vision of delivering mankind from spiritual oppression. See the Scripture below for your enlightenment:

> And the scroll of the prophet Isaiah was handed to him. Unrolling it, he found the place where it is written: "The Spirit of the Lord is on me, because he has anointed me to proclaim good news to the poor. He has sent me to proclaim freedom for the prisoners and recovery of sight for the blind, to set the oppressed free, to proclaim the year of the Lord's favor." Isaiah 61:1-2. (Luke 3:17-19, NIV)

The Call to Leadership: The Case of Moses

The lessons that today's leaders can learn from Moses' role in delivering the Israelites from Egyptian oppression are as follows:

1. A church leader's vision should contribute to the setting free of those who are under the bondage of the devil.
2. A corporate leader's work should contribute to the reduction of poverty and suffering in the world.

The leadership principle implicit in Moses' role is that of:

- Altruism.

5

The Call to Leadership
The Case of Paul

PAUL WAS CALLED PRIMARILY to be a minister of the gospel to the Gentiles. While he would preach mainly to the Gentiles, he was not to totally ignore the people of Israel, as indeed his ministry began there before moving further afield. See the Scripture below for further enlightenment:

> But the Lord said to Ananias, "Go! This man is my chosen instrument to proclaim my name to the Gentiles and their kings and to the people of Israel. " (Acts 9:15, NIV)

In another Scripture, Paul asserts that his vision or assignment from Jesus Christ is as follows:

> He gave me the priestly duty of proclaiming the gospel so that the Gentiles might become an offering acceptable to God, sanctified by the Holy Spirit. (Rom 15:16b, NIV)

Paul's call shows that for one to be a church or ministry leader, they should have been called and should also have received a specific mandate or assignment to go with their calling. Therefore, if one has been called by God, they also receive the mandate of their calling, because God calls people for different purposes

The Call to Leadership: The Case of Paul

or ends. Indeed some have been called to be visionary or overall leaders, while some have been called to be complementary leaders.

Visionary leaders are usually called to chart a new course in ministry or to take the work of the ministry to a different level or direction. Paul's call was that of a visionary leader, as he would chart a new course in history, by extending the gospel to the Gentiles or to the world.

The lessons that today's leaders can learn from Paul's call are as follows:

1. For one to be a leader, they ought to have been called.
2. When called by God, a leader is also given their specific assignment or vision.
3. Leaders are given or should demand specific job mandates for the avoidance of doubt.
4. In the marketplace, leaders also join leadership at different levels.

The leadership principle implicit in Paul's call is:

- Role clarity.

Paul displayed exemplary leadership and total commitment to his call by immediately embracing his call as shown in the Scripture cited below:

> But when God, who set me apart from my mother's womb and called me by his grace, was pleased to reveal his Son in me so that I might preach him among the Gentiles, my immediate response was not to consult any human being. (Gal 1:15–16, NIV)

The lessons that today's leaders can learn from Paul's stance on his call are as follows:

1. When one has been called to God's work, they should immediately embrace their call.
2. Leaders in the circular world should also focus on their core business in order to realise their set goals.

Template for Leadership

One should remain faithful to their call and not allow others to divert them from their God-given vision.

The leadership principles implicit in Paul's stance on his call are the following:

- Responsiveness.
- Commitment.
- Focus.

When Paul was called, he responded to his call by immediately embarking on the work for which he had been called, beginning in Damascus from where he had been called; thereby providing a good example for anyone who would have been called.

Paul also displayed commitment to his assignment through his above-cited assertion that he had been sent to preach the gospel to the Gentiles. If a leader is committed to their call, they should never consult other people, lest they get diverted from their vision since God calls people for specific purposes. If a leader gets diverted from their vision or core business, they never get rewarded as they would have departed from their vision. Leader commitment also results in positive energy that energises others to emulate their good example.

Furthermore, anyone who focuses on their core business sets themselves up for success, because they avoid all programmes and activities that do not feed into their given vision.

While Paul was called to be a visionary leader, Barnabas was called to complement and support him. In other words, Barnabas had the spiritual gift of "Helps" that was manifested through his ability to the effectiveness of Paul's ministry. And in line with that calling, he persuaded the disciples in Jerusalem, who were sceptical of Paul's conversion, to accept him, by relating the Damascene encounter and how Paul had preached fearlessly in the name of Jesus. See the Scripture below for further details:

> But Barnabas took him and brought him to the apostles. He told them how Saul on his journey had seen the Lord and that the Lord had spoken to him and how in

The Call to Leadership: The Case of Paul

Damascus he had preached fearlessly in the name of Jesus. (Acts 9:27, NIV)

People can also be called to complementary leadership as shown by Barnabas' call recorded in the Scripture below:

> While they were worshipping the Lord and fasting, the Holy Spirit said, "Separate for me Barnabas and Saul for the work for which I have called them." (Acts 13:2, NIV)

After their call, the respective roles of Paul and Barnabas were confirmed and demonstrated at Lystra. After the preaching of the gospel and the healing of a lame man at Lystra, the audience thought the two were gods and gave them names befitting their respective roles, according to the Scripture cited below:

> When the crowd saw what Paul had done, they shouted in the Lycaonian language, "The gods have come to us in human form!" Barnabas they called Zeus, and Paul they called Hermes because he was the chief speaker. (Acts 14:11–12, NIV)

The Lystra incident served to confirm unequivocally the relative leadership roles of Paul and Barnabas. Paul was the main speaker (top leader), while Barnabas was the complementary leader who was probably responsible for making introductory remarks, before handing over to the former.

The lessons to be learnt by today's leaders from Paul's and Barnabas' complementary roles are as follows:

1. If you have the calling for overall leadership, God will raise others to support and complement you.
   God will not send you alone.

2. Leaders should stick to their respective mandates for the avoidance of confusion.

The leadership principles implicit in the work set up of Paul and Barnabas are the following:

- Participation.

Template for Leadership

- Building synergies.
- Role clarity.

The participation of others in leadership, takes off the burden from one person while also building relevant synergies, which result in better work outcomes. Role clarity among the leaders ensures harmonious coexistence among them. It also ensures that all tasks are done, since leaders at all levels should stick to their mandates.

Paul also underlined the significance of complementarity leadership in the Scripture cited below:

> I planted the seed, Apollos watered it, but God has been making it grow ... The one who plants and the one who waters have one purpose and they will each be rewarded according to their own labor. For we are co-workers in God's service, you are God's field, God's building. (Romans 3: 6, 8–9, NIV)

The above was Paul's response to resolve a dispute regarding who was the legitimate leader between himself and Apollos. He resolved the dispute by pointing to the real leader (God) in a show of humility and by asserting that he and Apollos were mere co-workers, who complemented each other, in the building of the church of Christ.

Paul asserted that he planted the seed (carried the vision of and laid the foundation of the Gentile church) while Apollos watered (nurtured it complementarily) to show that leadership is indeed a shared vocation.

Paul's humility was shown by his attitude towards Apollos whom he regarded as his equal (co-worker), although the former was the visionary leader of the Gentile church, while the latter was one among many complementary leaders.

The lessons to be leant by today's leaders in respect of Paul's attitude towards Apollos are as follows:

1. Leaders complement one another.
2. Leaders should have unity of purpose and work as partners to achieve one end.

3. Leaders should be humble.

The leadership principles implicit in respect of Paul's attitude towards Apollos are the following:

- Building synergies.
- Unity of purpose.
- Humility.

As all the leaders actively work together, useful synergies are created, that result in more robust outcomes than would have been the case if they acted independently of each other, and in an uncoordinated manner.

Paul also shows that leaders should have unity of purpose-an attribute borrowed from the Godhead-when he says, ". . . the one who plants and the one who waters have one purpose." The one purpose that overall and complementary leaders have is to work in God's field or to build his church complementarily, through their diverse contributions. This immediately brings into focus the distinction between management and leadership; where in the former, position and rank are emphasised, while in the latter, equality and idiosyncratic contribution are the defining factors.

Humility is indeed an attribute that is required of visionary leaders in order to attract buy-in from complementary leaders. Of course, humility is required of leaders at any level for them to become acceptable to their followers, resulting in the latter's loyalty to the former.

Good leaders should lead by example as Paul did. His commitment to exemplary leadership is encapsulated in his assertion to the Corinthian church that he "walked the talk," demonstrating to others the way to go. See the Scripture below for further enlightenment:

> I persevered in demonstrating among you the marks of a true apostle, including signs, wonders and miracles. (2 Cor 12:12, NIV)

In a sense, Paul was calling on the church in Corinth to live lives worthy of their Christian calling.

Template for Leadership

His exemplary leadership is further demonstrated when he urged the church members at Thessalonica to emulate his example of diligence, in the Scripture cited below:

> For you know yourselves how you ought to follow our example. We were not idle when we were with you, nor did we eat anyone's food without paying for it. On the contrary we worked night and day, labouring and toiling so that we would not be a burden to any of you. We did this, not because we do not have the right to such help, but in order to offer ourselves as a model for you to imitate. (2 Thess 3:7–9, NIV)

Paul also exhorted the leaders at Ephesus to generosity, by referring to his own example in the Scripture below:

> You yourselves know how these hands of mine have supplied my own needs and the needs of my companions. In everything I did, I showed you that by this kind of hard work, we must help the weak, remembering the words of the Lord Jesus himself who said, "It is more blessed to give than to receive." (Acts 20:34–35, NIV)

The lessons that today's leaders can learn from Paul's exemplary leadership are as follows:

1. Leaders should be exemplary in the way they live their lives.
2. Leaders should practice what they teach.

The leadership principle implicit in Paul's example is that of:

- Integrity.

Leaders who practice what they teach have a positive influence on their followers in that the latter are likely to emulate the former's good behaviour. Honest leaders or leaders with high integrity become more acceptable to their followers thereby gaining their acceptance and loyalty.

Paul's ministry shows that leaders should persevere in the face of hardship and persecution. His exemplary leadership in this regard was played out at Lystra, where he was stoned and dragged

The Call to Leadership: The Case of Paul

out of the city, but still came back. See the Scripture below for more details:

> Then some Jews came from Antiock and Iconium and won the crowd over. They stoned Paul and dragged him out of the city, thinking he was dead. But after the disciples had gathered around him, he got up and went back into the city. (Acts 14:19, NIV)

Indeed those who have been called to leadership should know that the path of leadership is not a stroll in the park, as it is strewn with all kinds of trials and temptations.

Paul persevered to the end, as he was imprisoned on account of his calling at the instigation of the Jews. He appealed to Caesar, as God's design for him to also preach the gospel in Rome because it later became manifest that he had been commissioned to do so. See the Scripture below for your encouragement:

> The following night the Lord stood near Paul and said, "Take courage! As you have testified about me in Jerusalem, so you must also testify in Rome." (Acts 23:11, NIV)

To emphasise his perseverance and faithfulness to his calling, Paul asserted while being tried by King Agrippa, that he couldn't disobey his call, hence his arrest:

> So then, King Agrippa I was not disobedient to the vision from heaven. (Acts 26:19, NIV)

Paul was able to do so because he knew very well that our present sufferings counted for nothing compared with our future glory in eternity, as he asserted in another Scripture that:

> I consider that our present sufferings are not worth comparing with the glory that will be revealed in us. (Rom 8:18, NIV)

The lessons that today's leaders can learn from Paul's exemplary leadership are as follows:

1. Leaders should persevere in the face of trials and tribulations.
2. Leaders should remain steadfast, no matter what.

Template for Leadership

The leadership principle implicit in Paul's example is that of:

- Steadfastness.

Leaders, who endure trials and temptations and remain steadfast in the face of any challenges, gain the admiration and loyalty of their followers because of their commitment to their calling. They also impart positive energy in that their example is likely to catch on with their followers. Leaders who persevere and remain steadfast will in due course reap a befitting reward in eternity. Steadfast leaders are 'goal-getters' since they do not shrink back from pursuing their goals, no matter what.

Moreover, those who have been called to church or ministry leadership should persevere in the face of trials and temptations, because they will be handsomely rewarded as the Scripture cited below shows:

> Look, I am coming soon! My reward is with me, and I will give to each person according to what they have done. (Rev 22:12, NIV)

In the business world, leaders who do not shrink back are more likely than not to achieve their goals, resulting in deserving promotion and or relevant financial rewards.

The disagreement between Paul and Barnabas concerning John Mark provides a clear illustration of the 'Do's' and 'Don'ts' of people in visionary and complementary leadership.

When Paul and Barnabas were about to pay another visit to the cities they had previously visited to check on how the believers were doing, they disagreed on the incorporation of Mark who had previously deserted them, leading to the two parting company, according to the Scripture cited below:

> Barnabas wanted to take John also called Mark, with them, but Paul did not think it wise to take him, because he had deserted them in Pamphylia and had not continued in the work. (Acts 15:37-38, NIV)

We learn from the above-mentioned Scripture that overall and complimentary leaders should play different, albeit

The Call to Leadership: The Case of Paul

complimentary roles. But when this general understanding was challenged by Barnabas, they parted ways with their preferred aides. Below is the relevant Scripture on this subject:

> ... but Paul chose Silas and left, commended by the believers to the grace of the Lord. (Acts 15:40, NIV)

The lessons for today's leaders emanating from Paul's and Barnabas's disagreement regarding John Mark are as follows:

1. There is division of labor among leaders.
2. The overall leader carries the vision of the ministry or organisation and should therefore have the final word on issues pertaining to execution of that vision
3. Complementary leaders should submit to visionary leaders just as visionary leaders submit to God.
4. God will always raise complementary leaders to replace those who would have 'abandoned the post.'

The leadership principles implicit in the story of Paul and Barnabas are the following:

- Role clarity.
- Submission.

Where visionary and complementary leaders are clear about their respective roles, there is harmony between them. Since complementary leaders have been called to support the visionary leaders, they are expected to submit to the final word of the latter on issues pertaining to the execution of any God-given vision. And because God is faithful, desiring to see his vision through, he will always raise a replacement for complementary leaders who would have left. This should be a source of inspiration to visionary leaders that their vision will eventually be accomplished in spite of temporary setbacks.

Paul, following the footsteps of our Lord and Saviour Jesus Christ, was a strong believer in sacrificial leadership, as he

Template for Leadership

prioritised the needs of others over his own, by advising the leaders of the church at Ephesus as follows:

> Keep watch over yourselves and the flock of which the Holy Spirit has made you overseers. Be good shepherds of the church of God which he bought with his own blood. (Acts 20:28, NIV)

In line with sacrificial leadership, Paul was prepared to forego his freedom in order to preach the gospel of Jesus to the Gentiles, as he asserted to the church at Philippi, that:

> Now I want you to know brothers and sisters that what has happened to me has actually served to advance the gospel. As a result it has become clear throughout the palace guard and to everyone else that I am in chains for Christ. (Phil 1:12–13, NIV)

Paul's sacrificial leadership is revealed by his apt exhortation to the Philippians to imitate Christ's selflessness. See the Scripture cited below for further details:

> Do nothing out of selfish ambition or vain conceit. Rather in humility, value others above yourselves, not looking to your own interests but each of you to the interests of the others. In your relationships with one another, have the same mind set as Christ Jesus. (Phil 2:3–4, NIV)

This Scripture is a revelation of Paul's selfless demeanour because the word of God teaches us that the mouth speaks what the heart is full of (Luke 6:45b).

To demonstrate sacrificial leadership, Paul, on his own behalf and also on behalf of his companions, asserted to the church in Corinth that:

> We do not peddle the work of God for profit. (2 Cor 2:17a, NIV)

The lessons that today's leaders can learn from Paul's sacrificial leadership are as follows:

The Call to Leadership: The Case of Paul

1. The essence of leadership is what one gives to and not what one gets out of ministry or one's position.
2. Leadership involves foregoing one's comfort and or interests for the benefit of others.
3. Leadership should not be abused for the sake of acquiring dishonest gain.

The leadership principles implicit in Paul's example cited above are the following:

- Selflessness.
- Integrity.

A selfless leader gains the admiration, acceptance and loyalty of his/her followers. They also become a source of inspiration for others to emulate. Leaders with integrity do not use their positions to acquire dishonest gain, through such dubious schemes as 'seeding' and payment for one-on-one counselling sessions.

Paul's call to ministry-as should everyone's who has been genuinely called-mirrored Christ's vision of man's salvation, as revealed by the former when he appeared before king Agrippa, while narrating the details of his call. See the Scripture below for further details on how Paul mimicked Jesus' visionary leadership:

> I am sending you to open their eyes and turn them from darkness to light and from the power of Satan to God, so that they may receive forgiveness of sins and a place among those who are sanctified by faith in me. (Acts 26:17b–18, NIV)

The lesson that today's leaders can learn from Paul's visionary leadership is as follows:

1. The work of those who have been called to ministry should mimic that of Christ since they were called to extend his work on the earth.

The leadership principle implicit in Paul's imitation of Christ's vision is that of:

Template for Leadership

- Consistency.

The vision of Christian leaders should be consistent with that of Christ. It should idiosyncratically contribute to Jesus' general vision of man's redemption. This then clearly brands them as leaders who have been truly called since there is no confusion in the kingdom of God. In any other organisation, a leader's mandate should feed into the vision of that organisation. This has the effect of making leaders fit for purpose.

Paul's ministry was also marked by servant leadership, as he clearly asserted in the Scripture cited below:

> For what we preach is not ourselves, but Jesus Christ as Lord, and ourselves as your servants. (2 Cor 4:5, NIV)

The lesson for today's leaders from Paul is as follows:

1. Leaders should seek to serve the interests of others.

The leadership principle implicit in Paul's attitude is that of:

- Service.

A leader who is prepared to serve others receives people's acceptance and loyalty. Leaders, who are prepared to have their hands dirty, exude positive energy that influences others to do likewise, leading to a higher probability of success for the organisation.

Paul practised exemplary leadership through his good social skills-as any good leader should—that endeared him to his followers. Paul was fatherly and comforted those in distress. He also taught gentle correction for those who would have been found living ungodly lives. See the Scriptures below for further details:

> For you know that we dealt with you as a father deals with his own children, encouraging , comforting and urging you to live lives worthy of God, who calls you into his kingdom and glory. (1 Thess 2:11–12, NIV)

> Brothers and sisters, if someone is caught in a sin, you who live by the Spirit should restore that person gently. (Gal 6:1, NIV)

The Call to Leadership: The Case of Paul

If Paul was fatherly, as mentioned in the above-mentioned biblical passage, then he should also have been caring and concerned about how church members were doing, just as a loving father would. And by comforting those in distress and gently correcting church members, Paul was demonstrating fatherly love that should motivate leaders even today; because leaders, who genuinely love people and gently correct them, receive love in return since love is like a boomerang that always comes back to you!

1 Thessalonians 2:11–12 also shows that Paul must also have had an open-door policy, as a father is approachable and accessible to his children. Therefore, good leaders should display good social skills in order to earn the trust and loyalty of their followers.

The lessons that today's leaders can learn from Paul's example are as follows:

1. Leaders should have genuine love for people.
2. Leaders should be concerned about how their followers are doing.
3. Good leaders should point the right way to go for their followers.
4. Good leaders should correct their followers gently.

The leadership principles implicit in Paul's exemplary leadership are the following:

- Caring.
- Tactfulness.

Caring for how their followers are doing, in a church context, implies that leaders should be concerned about their followers' eternity by encouraging them to live righteous lives. Caring leaders receive the acceptance and loyalty of their followers. Tactful church leaders retain followers through gentle correction.

In all fields of human endeavour, caring leaders are concerned with how their subordinates are performing their roles. They should also correct them gently and this has the potential of fostering industrial harmony and high productivity in the organisation.

Template for Leadership

The above-mentioned attributes of leadership stamp one as a true leader, because leadership is defined more by the influence one exerts on their followers than merely their position in the organisation.

6

The Call to Leadership
The Case of Joshua

JOSHUA WAS CALLED TO take over from Moses-who had died-in order to lead the Israelites into the Promised Land, thereby taking over Moses' visionary leadership. God also urged Joshua to be courageous and strong i.e. fearless during his military campaigns, as he was assured of victory over all the nations he was going to dispossess of their land. See the Scripture below for the details:

> Moses my servant is dead. Now then you and all these people, get ready to cross the Jordan River into the land I am about to give them-to the Israelites . . . No one will be able to stand against you all the days of your life. As I was with Moses, so I will be with you. I will never leave you nor forsake you . . . Be strong and courageous. Be careful to obey all the law my servant Moses gave you; do not turn from it to the right or to the left, that you may succeed wherever you go. (Josh 1:2; 5, 7, NIV)

The lessons that today's leaders can learn from Joshua's story are as follows:

1. To go into church or ministry leadership one should have been called to do so.

2. God's vision for church or ministry leadership will never die even though individuals may die.
3. If a leader dies, God raises another to carry the vision forward.
4. Church or ministry leaders should know that God's purpose will always prevail in spite of the intensity of any opposition.
5. As long as one continues meticulously following God's commands for their calling, they will succeed in accomplishing their vision for the ministry.
6. Even in other fields of human endeavour, leaders who remain faithful to their core business will always succeed.

The leadership principles implicit in Joshua's call are the following:

- Commitment.
- Faithfulness.

Commitment is of crucial importance to leaders, in that for them to achieve their goals and objectives; they should persevere in spite of any obstacles they may encounter along the way. Faithfulness to one's call or core business is also a good recipe for success.

Leaders should have faith in God's direction and meticulously follow the leading of the Holy Spirit in order to achieve their goals and objectives, just as Joshua received the strategies from God for the Jericho and Ai military campaigns. He succeeded because he had faith in God's instruction which he then followed faithfully. In regard to the Jericho campaign, see the Scripture cited below:

> Then the LORD said to Joshua, "See I have delivered Jericho into your hands along with its king and its fighting men. March around the city once with all the armed men. Do this for six days. Have seven priests carry trumpets of rams' horns in front of the ark. On the seventh day, march around the city seven times with the priests blowing the trumpets. When you hear them sound the long blast on the trumpets, let the whole army give a loud shout; then the wall of the city will collapse and the army will go up, everyone straight in." (Josh 6:2–5, NIV)

The Call to Leadership: The Case of Joshua

And regarding the capture of Ai, God used the javelin in Joshua's hand to accomplish the task:

> Then the LORD said to Joshua, "Hold out toward Ai, the javelin that is in your hand, for into your hand I will deliver the city." So Joshua held out toward the city the javelin that was in his hand. As soon as he did this the men in the ambush rose quickly from their position and rushed forward. They entered the city and captured it and quickly set it on fire. (Josh 8:18–19, NIV)

The lessons that today's leaders can learn from the Jericho and Ai military campaigns are as follows:

1. God's call to leadership is also accompanied by his direction.
2. If a leader faithfully follows God's direction in ministry, they will always succeed.
3. In general, a leader who faithfully sticks to his/her core business will also succeed in whatever they do.

The leadership principles implicit in the Jericho and Ai campaigns are the following:

- Faithfulness (to one's calling).
- Faith (in God's direction).

Therefore, if one has been called to ministry leadership, he/she should never hesitate to embrace their call, because God will always direct their path. Faithfulness to one's call or core business always breeds success.

Complementary leadership was also played out when Joshua was called to complement Moses by completing the latter's call to take the Israelites to Canaan, after the latter had died. This development also served to demonstrate the principle of leadership continuity.

Again, Joshua proved to be a faithful complementary leader in respect of Moses' vision, since he scrupulously adhered to the command given to Moses to kill all the people and only carry off

Template for Leadership

plunder and livestock when conducing military campaigns in Canaan. See the Scriptures below for your enlightenment:

> The Israelites carried off for themselves all the plunder and livestock of these cities, but all the people he put to the sword until he completely destroyed them, not sparing anyone that breathed. (Josh 11:14, NIV)

> As the LORD commanded his servant Moses, Moses commanded Joshua, and Joshua did it: he left nothing undone of all that the LORD commanded Moses. (Josh 11:15, NIV)

The lessons that today's leaders can learn from Moses and Joshua's complementarities are as follows:

1. Complementary leaders can carry forward a leader's vision after their own departure, showing that leadership should be a continuous process.
2. Complementary leaders should meticulously run with the vision defined by the visionary leader after the latter's demise or departure.

The leadership principles implicit in Joshua's leadership are the following:

- Continuity (of leadership).
- Faithfulness (to the existing vision).

For optimal performance, gaps in leadership should never be entertained in any organisation. Top church or ministry leaders should also train and groom potential future leaders from the pool of existing potential leaders to foster faithfulness to God's vision for the purpose of continuity.

Joshua demonstrated exemplary leadership by leading by example during the renewal of the covenant at Shechem. See the Scripture below for more details on the above-mentioned issue:

> But if serving the LORD seems undesirable to you, then choose for yourselves this day whom you shall serve,

The Call to Leadership: The Case of Joshua

whether the gods your ancestors served beyond the Euphrates or the gods of the Amorites, in whose land you are living. But as for me and my household, we will serve the LORD. (Josh 24:15, NIV)

The lesson that today's leaders can learn from Joshua's exemplary leadership is the following:

1. Leaders should serve as good role models for their followers.

The leadership principle implicit in Joshua's leadership is that of:

- Credibility.

Credible leaders are faithful to their call through exemplary living. This earns them the loyalty of their followers because of their genuineness. It is this loyalty that then galvanises the entire organisation towards the achievement of organisational goals.

During the renewal of the covenant at Shechem, Joshua pointed the Israelites to acceptable behaviour, by reminding them that God had promised to fight for them, conquer their enemies, and give them the land of Canaan as their inheritance if they obeyed his commands and desisted from idolatry. By pointing the way to go, Joshua was demonstrating visionary leadership; as such leaders always remind others of the direction they should take.

Joshua displayed visionary leadership by declaring that he and his household would serve the Lord. Similarly, Joshua allowed for choice by asking the Israelites to choose between God and idols because he was a good leader.

The lessons that today's leaders can learn from Joshua's good leadership skills are as follows:

1. A good leader always reminds others about the founding vision of their organisation.
2. A good leader leads by example.
3. A leader suggests rather than dictates.
4. A leader is not a boss.

Template for Leadership

The principles implicit in Joshua's example are the following:

- Faithfulness (to the vision).
- Credibility.

Good leaders should 'walk the talk' by practising what they teach to ensure credibility, while also gently pointing the way their followers should go, without relying too much on authority, because a leader should not boss people around. Good leaders should also remain faithful to their calling. These values are crucial in that they ensure leader acceptability and follower buy-in.

7

The Call to Leadership
The Case of Joseph

THE STORY OF JOSEPH is a typology or shadow of what was to come: Jesus' humiliation and exaltation.

Joseph was born during his father's old age, which never represented a place of honour. Then he was thrown down the dry pit by his jealous brothers, who loathed the idea that Joseph was their father's favourite child as he was a child of his old age. Moreover, Joseph had had dreams in which he was their leader as an indicator of his future leadership role. See the Scriptures below for further details:

> Now Israel loved Joseph more than any of his sons because he had been born to him in his old age. (Gen 37:3a, NIV)

> Joseph had a dream and when he told it to his brothers, they hated him all the more. He said to them, "Listen to this dream I had: We were binding sheaves of grain out in the field when suddenly my sheaf rose and stood upright, while your sheaves gathered around mine and bowed down to mine." (Gen 37:5–7, NIV)

> Then Joseph had another dream, and he told it to his brothers. "Listen," he said, "I had another dream, and

Template for Leadership

this time the sun and moon and eleven stars were bowing down to me." (Gen 37:9, NIV)

Joseph was called to visionary leadership (being the executive prime minister) of Egypt who would save the Egyptians from starvation and the Israelites from possible extinction in due course. Of course, the Israelites had to be preserved since our Lord and Saviour would come through Jacob's lineage. Joseph's vision, mandate or assignment was that of being a 'preservatory' ruler (leader). One's mandate or assignment is called a vision or dream because it is usually relayed through a dream at night or through a vision seen when one is in a trance during daytime.

The lessons that today's leaders can learn from Joseph's story are as follows:

1. To be a leader one should have been called.
2. When a leader is called they are also given an accompanying vision or assignment.
3. Leaders in all fields of human endeavour should be given a clear mandate to focus on.

The leadership principle implicit in Joseph's call is that of:

- Being focussed.

A leader who remains faithful to their call—like Joseph—will always accomplish their vision. The important thing is for one to remain focussed and avoid being distracted from one's mandate. When Joseph was sent by his father to go and check on his brother's welfare; they conspired to kill him, yet it was not to be, because God's vision can never be killed. If one has a calling for leadership, it will come to pass if they remain focussed as God says in his word:

> What I have said, that I will bring about; what I have planned that I will do. (Isa 46:11b, NIV)

See the Scriptures below for further details on the conspiracy against Joseph by his brothers:

The Call to Leadership: The Case of Joseph

> "Here comes the dreamer!" they said to each other. "Come let's kill him and throw him into one of these cisterns and say that a ferocious animal devoured him. Then we will see what comes of his dreams". . . When Rueben heard this he tried to rescue him from their hands. "Let's not take his life," he said. "Don't shed any blood. Throw him into this cistern here in the wilderness, but don't lay a hand on him." Rueben said this to rescue him from them and take him back to his father. And they took him and threw him into the cistern. The cistern was empty; there was no water in it. (Gen 37:20–22; 24, NIV)

The dry pit experience was a very humbling one indeed. And so was being sold into Egyptian slavery: See the Scriptures below on these subjects:

> Judah said to his brothers, "What will we gain if we kill our brother and cover up his blood? Come let's sell him to the Ishmaelites and not lay our hands on him; after all he is our brother, our own flesh and blood." His brothers agreed. So when the Midianite merchants came by, his brothers pulled Joseph up out of the cistern and sold him for twenty shekels of silver to the Ishmaelites who took him to Egypt. (Gen 37:26–27, NIV)

The lessons that today's leaders can learn from Joseph's vision are as follows:

1. If one has a vision, the devil will fight them.
2. God's vision can never be extinguished.

The leadership principle implicit in Joseph's experience cited above is that of:

- Steadfastness.

Leaders who are steadfast do not waver in the face of challenges and opposition. And if they do not throw up their hands in despair, they will realise their vision or dream in due course.

Joseph's humiliation and persecution deepened when the Ishmaelite merchants resold him to Potiphar to be his house slave,

Template for Leadership

from where he was subsequently imprisoned on false charges of attempted rape orchestrated by the latter's wife, after he had rebuffed her sexual advances. See the Scriptures below for details regarding Joseph's snub of Potiphar's wife:

> But Joseph refused. "With me in charge," he told her, "my master does not concern himself with anything in the house; in the field everything he owns he has entrusted to my care. No one is greater in this house than I am. My master has not withheld anything from me except you, his wife. How then could I do such a wicked thing and sin against God?" (Gen 39:8–9, NIV)

Even though Potiphar's wife persisted in luring Joseph to sleep with her, the former still refused, until she resorted to the use of force, on a day when the household servants were out of the house, as Joseph was doing his household chores.

Potiphar's wife grabbed Joseph by his cloak, which he left in her hands as he ran out of the house. Frustrated by Joseph' refusal, Potiphar' wife decided on using the former's cloak as evidence against him and succeeded in having him thrown into prison, not knowing that his imprisonment would pave his way to the throne. See the Scripture below for more details on the plot against Joseph and his subsequent imprisonment:

> She kept his cloak beside her until his master came back home. Then she told him this story: "That Hebrew slave you brought us came to me to make sport of me. But as soon as I screamed for help, he left his cloak beside me and ran out of the house.". . . Joseph's master took him and put him in prison, the place where the king's prisoners were confined. (Gen 39:16–18; 20, NIV)

The lessons that today's leaders can learn from Joseph's trials and tribulations are as follows:

1. If one has a calling to greatness or leadership, the devil will bring up trials and temptations to try to distract them from their vision.

The Call to Leadership: The Case of Joseph

2. If one remains faithful to their call and shuns sin or distractions, they will reach the pinnacle of their calling.

The leadership principle implicit in Joseph's trials and temptation is that of:

- Being focussed.

If a leader remains focussed on his vision or core business, neither trials, tribulations nor imprisonment can extinguish their God-given dream. So it was with Joseph when Potiphar's wife tried to tempt him to sleep with her and when he was imprisoned. Ironically, however, it was through his incarceration, during which period he accurately interpreted the dreams of Pharaoh's chief cupbearer and chief baker that paved the way for Joseph's exaltation to the throne as the second in command of the entire nation of Egypt. Joseph's exaltation came after he had interpreted Pharaoh's dreams at the recommendation of the latter's chief cupbearer.

God used the doom and gloom of imprisonment to create opportunities that would catapult him to the throne, as it is written:

> And we know that in all things, God works for the good of those who love him, who have been called according to his purpose. (Rom 8:28 NIV)

While in prison, Joseph accurately interpreted the dreams of Pharaoh's chief cupbearer and chief baker and this later led to Joseph's exaltation to the throne. See the Scripture below for further details:

> So the chief cup bearer told Joseph his dream. He said to him, "In my dream I saw a vine in front of me, and on the vine were three branches. As soon as it budded it blossomed, and its clusters ripened into grapes. Pharaoh's cup was in my hand and I took the grapes, squeezed them into Pharaoh's cup and put the cup into his hands." (Gen 40:11, NIV)

Joseph interpreted the chief cup bearer's dream and also urged him to throw in a good word about him with Pharaoh once he had been released as this would also pave the way for his own release. See the Scripture below for more details:

> This is what it means," Joseph said to him. "The three branches are three days. Within three days Pharaoh will lift up your head and restore you to your position and you will put Pharaoh's cup in his hand, just as you used to do when you were his cup bearer. But when all goes well with you, remember me and show me kindness; mention me to Pharaoh and get me out of this prison." (Gen 40:12–14, NIV)

The chief baker also related his dream to Joseph. He had had a dream in which he was carrying three baskets of bread stacked on top of each other, with birds eating out of the top basket. Joseph interpreted his dream as follows:

> "This is what it means," Joseph said: "The three baskets are three days. Within three days, Pharaoh will lift off your head and impale your body on a pole. And the birds will eat away your flesh." (Gen 40:18–19, NIV)

Today's leaders can learn some lessons from Joseph's experience as follows:

1. The right contacts and or social networks will take you to your dream.
2. If one has a dream, they should break out of their cocoon and embrace useful contacts and or networks to facilitate its realisation.

The leadership principle implicit in Joseph's interactions with the chief cupbearer and chief baker is that of:

- Being approachable.

A leader who is approachable is likely to engage others meaningfully and to receive recommendations that may eventually pave the way to their own promotion.

Two years after the chief cupbearer was released from prison, Pharaoh had two dreams that worried him profoundly. In the first

The Call to Leadership: The Case of Joseph

one, Pharaoh was standing by the river Nile; whereupon seven fat cows came out of the river and grazed among the reeds, followed by seven thin cows that also emerged out of the river to stand beside the fat ones. The seven thin cows then swallowed the fat ones. For a better appreciation of the above-mentioned dream, see the Scripture below:

> He was standing by the Nile, when out of the river there came up seven cows, sleek and fat, and they grazed among the reeds. After them, seven other cows, ugly and gaunt, came up out of the Nile and stood beside those on the riverbank. And the cows that were ugly and gaunt ate up the seven sleek, fat cows. (Genesis 41:1b–4a, NIV)

In the second dream, Pharaoh saw seven heads of good and healthy grain growing on a single stalk. After that seven thin heads of grain sprouted and swallowed the healthy ones. For a better appreciation of the above-mentioned dream, also see the Scripture cited below:

> He fell asleep again and had a second dream: Seven heads of grain, healthy and good, were growing on a single stalk. After them, seven other heads of grain sprouted—thin and scorched by the east wind. The thin heads of grain swallowed up the seven healthy, full heads. (Gen 41:5–7a, NIV)

When all the magicians and wise men of Egypt failed to interpret Pharaoh's dreams, his chief cup bearer recommended Joseph who had earlier on interpreted his own and the former chief baker's dreams accurately when they were in prison.

When Pharaoh sent for Joseph and said to him he had heard that the latter had the ability to interpret dreams, Joseph denied such ability and instead pointed to God-in humility-as the only one who was able to do so. See the following Scripture for your encouragement:

> Pharaoh said to Joseph, "I had a dream and no one can interpret it, but I have heard it said of you that when you hear a dream, you can interpret it." "I cannot do it,"

Template for Leadership

> Joseph replied to Pharaoh, "but God will give Pharaoh the answer he desires." (Genesis 41:15–16, NIV)

The lesson to be learnt by today's leaders from Joseph's example is as follows:

1. Leaders ought to be humble and give back the glory to God, where it rightfully belongs; as the following Scripture further encourages:

> No to us, LORD, not to us; but to your name be the glory for your love and faithfulness. (Ps115:1, NIV)

Another Scripture says:

> Humble yourselves before the LORD, and he will lift you up. (Jas 4:10, NIV)

Still another Scripture says:

> For all those who exalt themselves will be humbled, and those who humble themselves will be exalted. (Luke 18:14b, NIV)

The leadership principle implicit in Joseph's above-cited example is that of:

- Humility.

Humility endears people to everyone. And humble leaders are acceptable to their followers, leading to high staff morale and productivity. This will invariably lead to the leader being exalted.

Because he had humbled himself, Joseph was promoted that day to the position of executive prime minister, with Pharaoh remaining more or less a ceremonial king. This arrangement became the bedrock of the current governance structure where you may have an Executive Prime Minister and a ceremonial King or President.

Joseph interpreted Pharaoh's dreams as follows:

His dream of the seven fat cows that were swallowed by the seven thin cows was the same with that of the seven heads of good grain that were also swallowed by the seven heads of thin

The Call to Leadership: The Case of Joseph

grain. The meaning of the two dreams was that there would be seven years of bumper crops followed by another seven-year period of famine.

The apparent repetition of the above-mentioned dream, Joseph said, was a sign that God had firmly decided that it would certainly come to pass and that these developments would soon take place. Therefore, the dreams were meant for Pharaoh to prepare in advance, in order to avert the possibility of starvation among the people. See the Scriptures below for a better appreciation of these subjects:

"Then Joseph said to Pharaoh, ". . . the dreams of Pharaoh are one and the same . . . The seven good cows are seven years, and the seven heads of good grain are seven years . . . The seven lean, ugly cows that came up afterward are seven years, and so are the seven worthless heads of grain scorched by the east wind."

—Genesis 41:25a; 26a, 27a NIV;

"The reason the dream was given to Pharaoh in two forms is that the matter has been firmly decided by God, and God will do it soon."

—Genesis 41:32 NIV,

> And now let Pharaoh look for a discerning and wise man and put him in charge of the land of Egypt. Let Pharaoh appoint commissioners over the land to take a fifth of the harvest of Egypt during the seven years of abundance . . . This food should be held in reserve for the country, to be used during the seven years of famine that will come upon Egypt, so that the country may not be ruined by the famine. (Gen 41:33–34; 36, NIV)

The lessons to be learnt by today's leaders from Joseph's abilities are as follows:

1. Leaders should ask for anointing with the Spirit of wisdom, knowledge and discernment, because these are useful resources needed for one to reach the pinnacle of their calling.
2. Leaders need to cultivate relevant competencies to succeed in their leadership career.

Template for Leadership

The leadership principle implicit in Joseph's above-cited example is that of:

- Competency.

Leaders who are competent in their work get promoted. Leaders in the secular world can acquire competence through taking relevant training courses and through mentorship.

Joseph displayed competence when he interpreted Pharaoh's dreams and then suggested the appointment of a wise and discerning man to be in charge over the land of Egypt, along with commissioners who would be responsible for the collection of grain during the first seven years of plenty, and to distribute the same during the ensuing years of famine. It was this insightfulness, on the part of Joseph, that paved his way to the throne.

Pharaoh was intrigued by Joseph's wisdom to the extent of appointing him as the chief official or-in today's nomenclature-Executive Prime Minister, with the former being effectively relegated to the status of a more or less ceremonial Head of State. See the Scriptures below for further details:

> The plan seemed good to Pharaoh and his officials. So Pharaoh asked them, "Can we find anyone like this man, in whom is the spirit of God?" (Genesis 41:37–38, NIV)

> Then Pharaoh said to Joseph, "Since God has made all this known to you, there is no one so discerning and wise as you. You shall be in charge of my palace, and all my people are to submit to your orders. Only with respect to my throne will I be greater than you." (Gen 41:39–40, NIV)

Joseph's story has lessons for today's leaders as follows:

1. Anointed leaders are peculiar and stand out of the crowd.
2. The person who owns the vision should be the overall leader since he/she relates to it best and is therefore best suited to oversee its execution or implementation.

The Call to Leadership: The Case of Joseph

3. The other leaders will then run with the vision to support and complement the visionary leader.

The leadership principles implicit in Joseph's above-cited story are the following:

- Role clarity.
- Building synergies.

Where people are clear on their roles, they are likely to achieve their goals and where people work cooperatively in complementarity, they build synergies through the likelihood of non-overlapping deficiencies and or weaknesses in the team.

We may-generally speaking-coin the following 8 leadership aphorisms or sayings from Joseph's story:

- Humility precedes exaltation.
- Perseverance is a valuable resource for leadership, because if one wishes to ascend the throne, they should endure the lowly dry pit.
- Persecution leads to revelation.
- If one has been called to leadership, God makes it known to them.
- God always confirms his call.
- The way up is through going down.
- Anointed leaders stand out of the crowd.
- God lifts one up incrementally, until they reach the pinnacle of their career, as long as they remain faithful to their calling.

The following section of this chapter provides further details on the above-mentioned leadership aphorisms:

Humility precedes exaltation

See the following Scriptures for further encouragement on this subject:

> Humble yourselves, therefore, under God's mighty hand, that he may lift you up in due time. (1 Peter 5:6, NIV)

Template for Leadership

> For those who exalt themselves will be humbled and those who humble themselves will be exalted. (Matt 23:12b, NIV)

Perseverance is a valuable resource for leadership, because if one wishes to ascend the throne, they should endure the lowly dry pit

As mentioned above, the story of Joseph was a shadow of Jesus' humiliation and exaltation, as manifested in his own 'dry pit' and 'glory' moments. Jesus Christ's humiliation was paved by his unparalleled humility, in that though he was God, he came down to earth in the form of sinful man and was born in a manger in lowly Bethlehem of all places (Micah 5:2); faced false allegations that he was possessed by Satan (Beelzebul) to heal the sick and perform miracles and that he was claiming to be the earthly king of the Jews, leading to his arrest, ridicule, beatings and crucifixion that saved mankind from sin. Jesus then died and went down the grave, but after conquering death, he was exalted to the highest place in heaven and on earth and under the earth and also became the head of everything concerning the church. This is the reason why we pray in the name of Jesus.

By not protesting when being thrown down the dry pit by his brothers, Joseph served as a shadow of Jesus' silence in the face of his humiliation and suffering: a great display of humility.

The story of Joseph shows that if one accepts "dry pit" moments with humility, God can use the same to bring about revelation that will eventually take them to the throne.

While in the dry pit, Joseph must have humbled himself by putting his trust in the Lord for his deliverance. And while faced with false accusations from Potiphar's wife that led to his imprisonment, Joseph must have prayed (not cursed God for his predicament) for his deliverance as a sign of humility. It was this chain of events that resulted in revelation that paved Joseph's way to the throne.

Persecution leads to revelation

Dry pit moments serve to encourage and spur on those called to leadership, that when faced with adversity, they should turn to God; so that as they draw closer and closer to God (in humility),

The Call to Leadership: The Case of Joseph

he will provide the revelation that will eventually take them out of their 'dry pit' so that they achieve their vision.

If one has been called to leadership, God makes it known to them

Joseph's experience shows that when one is called, they become aware of it, as he asserted, when resisting temptation from Potiphar's wife as follows:

> No one is greater than I am. (Gen 39:9, NIV)

Joseph was able to make the above-mentioned assertion, because he knew he had been called to leadership. This is the reason why he could boldly declare that there was no one greater than him in Potiphar's house. This must have included Potiphar himself, although Joseph wasn't puffed up by this revelation.

God always confirms his call

Joseph's call to leadership can also serve to illustrate the fact that when one has been called to leadership, God always confirms it. In Joseph's case, we see that God called him through at least two dreams.

In the first dream, Joseph and his brothers were binding sheaves of grain in the field, whereupon his sheaf suddenly stood upright and those of his brothers bowed down to it in the manner in which subjects show respect to their kings (Genesis 37:5–7).

In the second dream, Joseph saw the sun, moon and eleven stars bowing down to him.

The sun represented his father (or fathers); the moon, his mother (or mothers), while the eleven stars represented his brothers (or siblings in general) as he would later rule over all the families in the entire nation of Egypt.

Therefore, if one receives a call to church or ministry leadership, they should be cautious and not rush before receiving a word of confirmation. Indeed, many church and or ministry leaders all over the world, report receiving confirmation of their calling over and over again.

The way up is through going down

Joseph's story is a vivid illustration of the fact that if one wishes to go up (into leadership); they should go there by going

Template for Leadership

down (in humility). This aphorism applies to leaders in all fields of human endeavour.

Anointed leaders stand out of the crowd

In Genesis 41:39–40, Pharaoh acknowledged that Joseph possessed unique qualities suitable for leadership, implying that leaders should demonstrate leadership qualities that mark them out as genuine leaders as the Holy Spirit empowers them.

God lifts one up incrementally, until they reach the pinnacle of their career as long as they remain faithful to their call

Joseph's story is also an illustration of the fact that if one remains humble; perseveres and remains true to their calling without being side-tracked; God will lift them up incrementally, until they reach the peak of their career.

Joseph was first lifted up to lead in Potiphar's household; second, he was lifted up to head a group of families represented by the prison community, before becoming leader of the entire nation of Egypt.

So at whatever level a leader finds themselves, if they persevere, serve faithfully, and remain humble, God will lift them up until they reach the pinnacle of their calling.

A Valedictory Note

I WISH TO REFRESH your mind a little bit by way of a concise recapitulation. Leadership approaches can be divided into two: participative and non-participative. Although this is the case, in this book, only the former approach is dealt with; since godly leadership is participative as revealed in this book.

Five leadership styles have been identified from biblical best practice cited in this book. The five leadership styles are: visionary, complementary, sacrificial, servant and exemplary leadership. Furthermore, a host of leadership best practices have been identified in order to guide the reader on good leadership practices they may be able appropriate for themselves.

Some eight leadership aphorisms or sayings have also been coined-emanating from the story of Joseph-to motivate the aspiring or practising leader to move along desirable leadership directions.

Last, but not least, around forty leadership principles underlying best leadership practices, gleaned from biblical case studies are provided, in order to equip the practising and or aspiring leader with the requisite leadership guidance.

It is therefore my fervent hope and prayer that as you navigate your God-given leadership career; you stand guided by the word of God and by the revelation of the Holy Spirit. Amen.

Bibliography

Boal, Kimberly B., and Robert Hooijberg. "Strategic Leadership Research: Moving On." *The Leadership Quarterly* 11.4 (2001) 515–49.
Bruce, J. Avolio, et al. "Leadership: Current Theories, Research and Future Directions." *Annu. Rev. Psychol* 60 (2009) 421–49.
Daft, Richard L. *The Leadership Experience*. 4th ed. Mason, OH: Southwestern Cengage, 2008.
Ireland, R. Duane, and Michael A. Hitt. "Achieving and Sustaining Strategic Competitiveness in the 21st Century: The Role of Strategic Leadership." *Academy of Management Perspectives* 19.4 (2005) 63–74.
Maxwell, John C. *The 5 Levels of Leadership: Proven Steps to Maximize Your Potential*. New York: Center Street, 2011.
The Holy Bible, King James Version. Uhrichsville, OH: Barbour, 2002.
The Holy Bible, New International Version. Grand Rapids: Zondervan, 2011.
Rowe, W. Glenn, and Mehdi Hossein Nejad. "Strategic Leadership: Short-term Stability and Long-term Viability." *Ivy Business Journal* (Sep/Oct, 2009).

www.ingramcontent.com/pod-product-compliance
Lightning Source LLC
Chambersburg PA
CBHW070511090426
42735CB00012B/2734